1.50

The mystery of telepathy

Joe Cooper

The mystery of telepathy

Constable · London

First published in Great Britain 1982
by Constable and Company Limited
10 Orange Street London WC2H 7EG
Copyright © 1982 by Joe Cooper
ISBN 0 09 464170 6
Set in Monophoto Baskerville 11pt by
Servis Filmsetting Ltd, Manchester
Printed in Great Britain by
St. Edmundsbury Press
Bury St. Edmunds, Suffolk

This book is dedicated to three pioneers of
thought transference studies: Fred Myers,
Edmund Gurney, and William Barrett.

'Certain obscure facts have been knocking
at the door of human intelligence for
(in all probability) many centuries.'

Oliver Lodge (1894)

Contents

Illustrations

Introduction

The importance of telepathy lies not so much in the novelty of the mysterious transfer of thought from one human to another as in its implication; for if it can be demonstrated conclusively that humans can communicate with one another outside the five senses, then it follows that there may be more to us than the known mind and body adjusted to the everyday world of time and space. It may mean that there are other and unknown parts of ourselves capable of making conscious impressions from time to time.

This line of reasoning has appealed to many researchers in the past. Sir William Crookes, an outstanding physical scientist of the last century, for example, declared at the end of his days that were he to begin his parapsychological studies over again, he would start with telepathy. And there have been many others, such as Lodge, Barrett and Myers, who have emphasised the central importance of the topic in psychic circles.

This book attempts a fairly comprehensive examination of the subject, as opposed to the few pages of reference which it seems to merit in most occult works. My viewpoints have been largely historical, sociological, and theoretical: who said what and when, how various groups in society reacted to such information, and what possible explanations have been put forward to explain telepathy. These are complex matters, and I suppose I have not done much more than scratch the surface in the hope that my words may stimulate imaginations if not the desire to study the subject further.

I have also tried to represent the views of materialistic critics of the subject as well as those of spiritual optimists who make up the bulk of the enthusiastic researchers. H.H. Price, an eminent philosopher, once observed that telepathy is something which ought not to happen if materialism is true. 'But it does happen,' he wrote, 'so there must be something seriously wrong with the Materialistic theory'.

But critics and champions both have their parts to play in research: the former undoubtedly serve to sharpen investigating techniques and the latter are ever questing for new data. Between them they may add to knowledge on the subject; aided, perhaps, by a book such as this which aims at a sympathetic and synthetic approach to a topic which most of us have always known about and some of us have endlessly pondered upon. May my words add to your interest and prompt further speculations beyond my own.

PART ONE

Preliminaries

Public wonder and scientific scepticism

In a sharp criticism of spiritualism written in 1921, the philosopher Edward Lawrence drew attention to man's tendencies to be ruled by feelings rather than logic when he wrote: 'As a creature of emotion, he has an immeasurable past; as a creature of reason, he is only of yesterday'. This wisdom is borne out by only the briefest of glances at mankind's turbulent history where action and passion have generally held sway. It may be that humanity and reason are slowly intervening, but at personal levels we still follow our hearts in the main; and in fringe areas like telepathy – that strange process whereby words, ideas or emotions seem to pass from one to another without sensory mediation – our verdicts on its truth tend to be emotionally tinged, for there is much to be awed by and little to go on by way of accumulated evidence. Lawrence, of course, was writing after a fearful war, when many of the bereaved were prone to accept even the most banal of messages purporting to emanate from lost loved ones; and he suggested that both savage and civilized man exhibited about equal capacities for gullibility when confronted by the unexpected and the puzzling, especially when explanations were given in wondrous terms, perhaps involving gods, guides or mysterious forces as yet unknown.

When telepathy occurs spontaneously in everyday life, often in some family or friendship situation, it is often greeted with some sort of surprised pleasure; as at the recognition of the sudden presence of some lesser telepathic god, who has descended fleetingly to earth and momentarily shown his ancient face. It is felt that, for a moment, the edge of some greater causal framework has shown itself – some subtle mechanism usually remote from the tedious patterns of our rather predictable everyday lives. Whereupon there is often talk and speculation of more things in heaven and earth, and some sense of wonder is temporarily preserved.

At a public level the need to wonder, to be awed, to be entertained, is strong. Music-hall promoters, media men, and all manner of conjurors and magicians have all commercially exploited this demand for centuries, and modes of presentation have been subtle. Chaucer wrote of conjurors making flowers spring up in a meadow or causing vines to flourish; sixteenth-century magicians would perform the now-familiar trick of pulling yards of ribbons from the mouth, and travellers' tales described bodies being dismembered and reassembled miraculously, or the production of food, drink, birds and other livestock from thin air. Such feats are always applauded, for to produce a spectacle of wonder, whether by treachery or not, is a satisfying and entertaining happening.

The idea of presenting a demonstration of thought-transference as a spectacle of public entertainment does not seem to have made its appearance before the eighteenth century. In 1784, the internationally famous conjuror Pinetti took over the Haymarket theatre in London for the winter season, and performed to packed audiences. It is likely that Mesmer's notions of hypnotism and animal magnetism were beginning to infiltrate slowly from Europe, and first theories of extra-sensory perception were emerging. Pinetti would blind-fold his wife in a box and then pass among members of the audience exhibiting various borrowed items which she would identify to storms of excited applause.

Of the greatest importance in such a performance is the presentation. Consider the remarks of a carnival man named Mannix who wrote of his days as a telepathy performer in *Memoirs of a Sword Swallower*:

> There are literally hundreds of methods known to the magician for finding out what is in a sealed envelope. But the method itself is nothing; the manner in which it is presented is vital . . .

And of a husband-and-wife team known as the Moyers who practised thought-reading he wrote:

To the tip, the Moyers weren't sideshow performers doing an act. They were magicians in the tradition of Chaldea and Egypt. They were gratifying a human desire nearly as deep and basic as the sexual urge. The Moyers had the same direct contact with the tip that a medicine man has with a primitive tribe.

It is perhaps significant that Mannix refers to the audience as 'the tip', which brings to mind some slow-moving mass which is alternately decanted in and out of a tent, yielding revenue, and there to be amused and mystified. It is vitally important that the attention of such a gathering is firmly caught and held, for there might be unpleasant consequences for those who fail.

Yet once the emotional approval of an audience has been gained, its capacity for expressing its gullibility becomes immeasurable. Mannix wrote of the Moyers involving the audience in their thought-reading routine: 'would all of you please help Madame . . . concentrate . . . this is a very difficult . . . concentrate . . .' and Moyer would raise clenched fists as his partner held a paper slip to her forehead, which she had already read off through her fake blindfold. After an appropriately dramatic pause she would gasp out names of towns or relatives, to be enthusiastically endorsed by those who had scrawled the message and the audience in general.

Conjurors, variously called stage magicians or illusionists, are sometimes personified by grandiose titles (e.g. The Amazing Randi) and are generally tough and keen-minded individuals who have been swift to exploit the insatiable public appetite for the marvellous down the centuries. They also express and utilize their own personalities or presences so that an allegedly magical stage performance becomes a thrilling experience for both performer and audience alike.

One of the most formidable of stage magicians was Harry Houdini, born in New York towards the end of the last century, and capable of suggesting the wonderfully mysterious by his very appearance on any stage. He was a stark stoic, intensely competitive, and dedicated to his profession of illusionist. Will Goldston, his lifelong friend, described him thus:

I know of no other public performer who can grip a vast

The power of the eye
The idea of some magnetic force coming from the eye is
centuries old and in this photograph of Houdini presented to the
author's parents it is the eyes that command attention

miscellaneous audience by the power of personality as quickly and thoroughly as he can. It is a rare gift and must have helped him tremendously during his career.

Houdini made use of a telepathy act with his wife during his young days, employing a fake blindfold for Bess and a visual signalling and verbal code as he displayed objects among the audience; but he soon moved on to more spectacular effects, particularly involving thrilling escapes, often while heavily bound or manacled.

The spectacle and the arousing of expectant emotions were all important. At a police station he would be stripped and searched and thrust into a cell from which nobody had ever escaped, often with newspapermen present. He would be out within minutes. On many occasions the solution to his feat was to be found in the simplest of explanations – that of having an accomplice, often an inconspicuous individual, one Collins, a cabinet-maker and locksmith. Few will have heard of him or the parts he played, as described by Gresham in his biography of the escapologist:

> He could go along on a prison break and hide the required picks or key skillfully in the cell where his true role was often not suspected – he could pass as a member of the committee and so solidly respectable did he look that nobody took him for a showman. His hair was thin on top, he wore glasses, and his manner was unassuming and modest; few could guess that he was, in truth, the right arm of the great Self-Liberator.

At the heart of many impressive stage telepathy acts, of course, are accomplices of one sort and another. A third party, standing in the wings, observing through peepholes and communicating with a bandaged thought-receiver on stage is one example; others, more familiar, are stooges in the audience, proffering driving licences and corroborating numbers read off by the sensitive. Where spectacular feats of thought-reading involving transmissions over many miles with the parties separated there is obviously room for accomplices at both ends, perhaps signalling visually what pre-arranged set piece or other performance is to be played out. The activities of race-course tic-tac men, Morse code and semaphore signallers, and the multiplicity of possible combinations of hand and limb movements in conjunction with facial movements, indicate the considerable potential of telepathy codes. And because these latter have become the most highly published of trick telepathy explanations, accomplices and set pieces have been too often ignored. In the case of telepathy research, then, the first laboratory may be said to have been places of public entertainment where such an apparently magical process was to be found, bringing about an association between stage performances and fraudulent behaviour and also public gullibility.

It is only in the last hundred years that telepathy has come under the scrutiny of scientists, and naturally the feeling that there is some party trick to be explained by rational means springs to the mind of the serious investigator. Perhaps for this reason, many researchers have been somewhat conscious of the need to be seen to have taken precautions against any trickery; there has also been a tendency to present results in tabulated or statistical form, perhaps to reassure scientists that such an obscure matter as thought-transference may be demonstrated empirically and numerically, thus meeting critics on their own ground.

Of those few scientists who have given their time to telepathy research or appraisal, there is the customary division into sheep and goats, or believers in occult influences and those sceptical of such matters. In our twentieth century so far the doubters have generally tended to sway public opinion. 'A scientist measures and predicts' remarked the veteran naturalist Alfred Russell Wallace; this first stage of measuring telepathic performance has been but barely reached; and as for predicting the incidence of success, there have been few attempts and no patterns discerned.

Of all areas of scientific investigation, it would seem at first blush that telepathy research is one of the least profitable. Systematic sceptics have drawn attention to the glaring fact that in the overwhelming majority of humans it is impossible to transmit or receive thoughts solely by means of the will. Everyday experience endorses this. There is thus a case for saying that such cases as have been discovered might have been as a result of over-enthusiastic reporting, trickery, unconscious cues having been given, experiment design flaws, and statistical optimism of one sort and another. That such (often valid) criticism may be directed at the cases on record would seem to strike a death knell, and herald victory for the goats. After all, is anybody the worse off if telepathy research is discontinued?

A simple answer is that nobody knows. Futurology is also in its infancy, and human forecasts as to the potential of any developing field of activity are often wildly askew. H.G. Wells thought there little future for aviation. Sir Walter Scott thought the idea of illuminating London by gas flames preposterous. Radio, film, and television were all thought of as little more than passing novelties in their early days, and Condorcet forecast that 'wars and revolutions will be less frequent' in 1784 (he himself died in the Reign of Terror).

Certainly the zeal of the Society for Psychical Research (S.P.R.) pioneers of the 1880s gradually became dessicated into endless dice and card and drawing experiments of the following half century or so. Orthodox science cast a long shadow over research designs in telepathy, and it was left to statisticians in the main to decide whether a particular telepathy hypothesis was tenable. In vain might the more thoughtful researchers claim that telepathic capacities were found among the more sensitive and that to expect people to exhibit such a capacity in laboratory conditions was akin to asking Keats or Shelley to compose to order under stop-watching observers. Hence the occasional critical studies by conventional investigating scientists tend to concentrate on possibilities of trickery, inaccurate reporting, a wish to believe in wonders, which distorts judgement, and critical scrutiny of masses of statistical findings which report successes beyond chance.

One such writer is the psychologist Professor Hansel, who dealt thoroughly with card guessing at Duke University, North Carolina, in the 1930s and experiments carried out by S.G. Soal a decade later, particularly with reference to two telepathic Welsh schoolboys. These latter, he claimed, generally had access to visual cues; sometimes from each other and at other times from third parties who stood nearby – parallels with stage telepathy are clear here. He also quoted the opinion of the American investigator J.L. Kennedy who in 1938 had reviewed in detail a mass of experiments on card and picture guessing and suggested that sources of experimental error, such as visual and

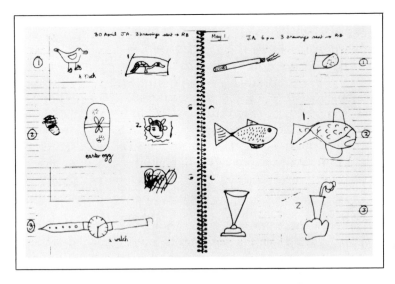

Telepathized drawings as reported by Professor Hasted

auditory cues, preferences for patterns in choosing and recording errors, could all lead to erroneous impressions of telepathy
taking place. Both Kennedy and Hansel advocated tighter test
conditions and Hansel pointed to the evidence of eighty-five
years and maintained that little progress had been made in
producing a repeatable experiment which would demonstrate
ESP for once and for all.

Yet it may be that scientific scepticism is becoming less sharp
in the last quarter of our century. John Hasted, professor of
experimental physics at Birkbeck College, University of
London, recently (1981) produced a closely written book called
The Metal Benders which gives abundant evidence of paranormal
phenomena. Here, indeed, is striking evidence of the power of
thought or imagination on metals and also much data on such
hitherto scoffed-at subjects as levitation, apports (the appearance of objects out of thin air) and 'informational psychic
phenomena' which includes the sending and receiving of
drawings. Hasted does not hesitate to write of his own casual
experiences in such experiments, and the tone of his descriptions
is in sharp contrast to the earlier tabulations and statistics of, say

SPR studies in the Thirties and Forties. The following extract would doubtless rile the present-day followers of Hansel and Kennedy, in that a measure of relaxation and even enjoyment is deemed necessary in such tests:

> My judgement is that the important thing about telepathy is its spontaneity. The mind of the telepathist at an unpredictable moment receives information and, with experience, he can sense that the information has not come to him through normal channels.

and:

> The most successful telepathy games that I have organized amongst metal-benders were played at a rate of three pictures each day after school. For a few days Richard B. was able to receive about 70 per cent of the pictures sent by my son John Andrew over a distance of ten miles.

It is perhaps worth noting that this distinguished author, who has worked all his life in atomic and molecular physics, does not shrink from confidently reporting family and personal occurrences to substantiate his views on the paranormal.

Such confidence in presentation was not experienced by the early researchers, such as Barrett and Myers, which led to their not debating fully and publicly much of the rich data on telepathy which had accumulated. Selfconsciously in the shadow of materialistic Victorian science, they took up apologetic stances and the role of explainers rather than pioneers.

A first step in considering telepathy has been to sample some attitudes from public and scientific viewpoints. The whole subject has alway been fraught with wonder and expounded by charlatans; only comparatively recently have scientists considered it seriously, and the first half of this century saw research dominated by critics and dessicated into marginally significant successions of tedious card guessing and drawing at a distance. Generally, telepathy became discredited academically.

A next move might be to consider telepathy researchers in relation to the times in which they lived and theories generated; so that we may once more journey over their findings and ideas, applying the yardsticks of caution used by the sceptics, but not neglecting the possibility that the wonderful may have been buried by social pressures somewhere along the way. For, as in all other human activities, we will find there were imperfections; there were misreportings and accurate records; there was modesty and vainglory; there were emotional commitments to this or that creed and the deep resultant need to confirm such from collected evidence; and there was the odd discovery, the surprising result, or even the incredible. It has been said that the true gold of research is often found in the unexpected and, with this aphorism somewhere in the background, we might now pass to a consideration of the adventures of long-dead scientists and scholars who sought to demonstrate the reality of telepathy.

[2]

Early researchers: scholars and scientists

At first sight it would seem that the second half of the nineteenth century was indeed an opportune time for psychical research and thus for telepathy investigation. Church doctrines, unopposed for centuries, were coming under attack from radicals and Darwinists alike; in the booming universities philosophers argued endlessly as to principles of social justice and the Nature of Man as the roots which were to lead to twentieth-century religions and political upheavals began quietly to spread.

There had also been a mass of psychic phenomena reported from many parts of the world, and it seemed that systematic and sustained studies might well lead to the firm establishment of a new body of knowledge connected with the non-material components of mankind. At Trinity College, Cambridge, classical scholars, Frederic Myers, Edmund Gurney and Henry Sidgwick, combined with Oxford-educated civil servant Frank Podmore to form the Society for Psychical Research in 1882, and the scientists Crookes, Wallace, William Barrett and Sir Oliver Lodge spent much of their spare time in gathering data on matters parapsychological.

But these early researchers came under heavy attacks from established scientific quarters from the very beginning. For the prevailing climate of Victorian England, based on half a century of successful industrial innovation and expansion both at home and in most parts of the world, had bred a materialistic and traditional attitude which is revealed in the lines of Kipling:

Walk wide of the widow of Windsor
For half of creation she owns.

Established and formidable science, represented by Huxley and

Faraday, spoke out strongly against the so-called wonders of the seance room, so that the founders of the SPR were, from the beginning, almost self-consciously aware of the need to demonstrate the rigour of their experimental work and critical attitudes towards those who reported occult data.

As it happened, the founding members or the SPR were badly shaken by events in the first ten years of the society's existence. The Creery sisters, tested by Barrett and others in telepathic experiments, were caught cheating after the publication of seemingly significant results. Gurney committed suicide in 1888 at the age of forty-one, perhaps after discovering that other seemingly genuine telepathists (Smith and Blackburn) were less than genuine; the documentation of his major work *Phantasms of the Living* (1887) had also been queried; and Podmore was to die in mysterious circumstances in 1910, with Myers going before his time at the age of fifty-seven in 1901. Conventional social pressures upon their unorthodox opinions may well have shortened their lives. Even a century later they are still attacked. Consider these robust comments by the distinguished psychiatrist, Elliot Slater, in his introduction to Trevor Hall's intriguing book *The Strange Case of Edmund Gurney*:

> Podmore was a poor pathetic creature who ended his life penniless, disgraced and drowned . . .
>
> Myers . . . was also a cold hearted egoist, who loved no one but himself. He was a liar and a coward, and he ran out on his friends when they were in trouble.

Three other scientists besides Barrett who conducted telepathy research were Crookes, Wallace and Lodge. They, too, suffered from public ridicule during their lives. Wallace was thought to be obsessed with spiritualism, and Lodge's book on the spirit survival of his son Raymond who was killed in the First World War and smoked cigars in the hereafter was ridiculed. Crookes suffered from subsequent disclosures by his former mediumistic researcher Florence Cook, and his views on telepathy were often discounted.

The opinions of early researchers have thus not been built upon; rather their research findings have been buried, and contemporary scientific opinion still looks askance at the subject, as has been shown in the first chapter. Perhaps, a hundred years after the founding of the SPR, the time has arrived for a reappraisal of their labours.

We might begin with a look at the major writings of the scholars – Myers, Gurney and Podmore. The three combined in the 1880s to produce the classic *Phantasms of the Living* which in spite of contemporary comments on the lack of letters backing up cases, is quoted freely in much psychic literature today. In its 1300 pages it not only marshals the evidence for telepathy later reproduced in *SPR Proceedings*, but also hundreds of cases where living, dying or dead persons are said to have appeared to others. All 702 cases are classified under the headings: percipient and agent, nature of impression (e.g. visual, emotional, in a dream), and the relationship of participants (e.g. friends, acquaintances, mother, brother etc.). Friends accounted for 31 per cent, for example, and the parent/child link was the most common bond. 58 per cent of those experiencing phantasms were female and 42 per cent male. The whole vast work puts a strong case for disembodied humans being able to make contact with the living. Myers summarised the main themes of this book simply:

1. Experiment proves that telepathy – the supersensory transference of thoughts and feelings from one mind to another – is a fact in nature.
2. Testimony proves that phantasms (impressions, voices, or figures) of persons undergoing a crisis – especially death – are perceived by their friends and relatives with a frequency which mere chance cannot explain.
3. These phantasms, then, whatever else they may be, are instances of the supersensory action of one mind on another.

Gurney also produced philosophical works, and Myers wrote poetry. Myers' major work was in two lengthy volumes entitled *Human Personality and Its Survival of Bodily Death* which was published posthumously in 1903. From Hall's provocative book on Gurney mentioned earlier he appears as a restless and egoistic person, but the medium Violet Tweedale took an opposite view:

F.W.H. Myers (1844–1901), a founder member of the Society for
Psychical Research

I remember the aura of Frederic Myers very well. A large and
intensely spiritual halo. He is the only man I can remember in
those days – about 92/96 – as having an aura within an aura,
though this phenomenon is becoming more marked.

'A rainbow was about his head' – those words explain

exactly what I mean. About a foot above his head circled a pure rainbow . . . I would assert that it stands for a certain initiation conferred upon 'the beloved' by the Masters of wisdom.

Frank Podmore, much maligned in modern times by critics such as Slater, at least achieved a mention in *Who's Who* and enjoyed something of a reputation as an impartial observer on matters psychic, for he became antagonistic to conventional spiritualism towards the end of his days. In his 1902 publication *Modern Spiritualism* he reveals many cases of fraud, doubtful testimony and mistaken perceptions, pointing out that the early pioneers gradually lost their enthusiasm and that 'in its later aspects Spiritualism had for some years ceased to attract men of like mind to replace them.' (Conan Doyle and Oliver Lodge, vigorous popularisers of the subject in the 1920s, had yet to come.)

Does his dislike of the seance room apply to telepathy? Podmore was cautious. Whereas he acknowledged its existence, he points to the patchy nature of the evidence and suggests that chance and coincidence must play parts in evaluating success rates. He also writes that:

Investigators have refrained from committing themselves to any theory of its mode of action . . . the power itself may be but a last relic of our discarded inheritance from the past, a long-disused faculty dragged from the dim lumber-room of primitive consciousness, and galvanized into a belated and halting activity . . .

The eminent scientist and fellow telepathy-researcher Sir William Barrett, writing after the mysterious death by drowning of Podmore on a rainy night in August 1910, paid cautious homage to his critical and historical abilities, but commented that 'he was chiefly known for his ingenuity in discrediting, or attributing to telepathy, psychical phenomena outside his limited range of view'.

What of the scientists? Did they fare any better than the classical scholars in producing significant early research findings on telepathy?

We might begin with William Barrett, who was born in 1844,

and became professor of physics at Dublin and distinguished for his activities to promote temperance, and for his magnetic and optical innovations, before dying at eighty-one in 1925 with much social honour. Throughout his life he had shown an interest in matters psychic, although in *SPR Proceedings*, Vol. 1, 1882, he declared his initial attitude towards telepathy in an appendix to the *Report on Thought Reading* thus:

> The inquiry must ultimately resolve itself into a question of evidence, and demands the exercise of the faculty of careful observation, which a physicist is as likely to possess as a physiologist.
>
> My own connection with the subject arose in this way. Some fifteen years ago, whilst staying with a friend in the country, I saw certain mesmeric experiments made on the children of one of my friend's tenants, which interested me greatly, in spite of my strong scepticism. Among other things, I noticed what appeared to be a transmission of impressions from the mind of the mesmeriser to that of the subject, without, so far as I could detect, any intervening sense of perception.

One or two interesting points emerge; first, Barrett had been interested in telepathy from 1867 onwards, when he was only a young man of twenty-three and at the height of his perceptive powers; secondly, he was a sceptic, and not a credulous believer looking for further evidence; and thirdly, he was well steeped in thought-transference experiments when he wrote a letter to *The Times* in 1876, nine years later, asking for further data from any sources. In this way he came to know Myers and Gurney, and worked closely with them from then on.

In 1881 the trio received a letter from the Reverend A.M. Creery of Buxton in Derbyshire, who claimed that each of his four young daughters, aged between eleven and seventeen was frequently able to designate correctly, without contact or sign, a card or other object fixed in the child's absence. Many experiments were carried out by Barrett, Myers and Gurney in the Creery household and these were later replicated by the scientists Professors Balfour, Stewart and Hopkinson. In some fifty of the latters' cases, for example, the guesser's back was turned to the company as the object or card was chosen during the experiment. From the choice of cards, objects and numbers results obtained were well beyond chance: correct first-time guesses accounted for 20 per cent and second or third correct for a slightly larger percentage: in summary, about half the cards, objects and two-digit numbers were discerned correctly when three guesses for each were made. Such a result certainly suggests some intervening mode of communication, perhaps at an extra-sensory level.

Barrett's figures were even more astonishing. It would be tedious to list results individually but, for one particular period in mid-April 1882, 382 trials were made in a period of six days. 'Of our trials,' wrote Barrett with astounding modesty,

> 127 were successes on the first attempt, 56 on the second and 19 on the third, making 202 in all . . . our most striking piece of success, *when the thing selected was divulged to none of the family*, was five cards running named correctly on the first trial; the odds against this happening once in our series was considerably over a million to one. We had a good many similar batches, the two longest runs being eight consecutive successes, once with cards and once with names; where the adverse odds in the former case were over 142 million to one and the latter something incalculably greater . . . the experimenters took every precaution in order that no indications, however slight, should reach the child. She was recalled by one of the experimenters and stood near the door with downcast eyes.

(The italics are mine.) All this is heavy stuff to counter the criticisms of sceptics who maintain that a signalling code was probably responsible for the high rates of success. Certainly in later experiments the girls had a signalling code for cards, but if the conditions were as stated by Barrett then no opportunities for cheating presented themselves.

Let our Dublin Professor William Barrett have the last word on the matter:

> On none of these occasions was it even remotely possible for the child to obtain by any ordinary means a knowledge of the

card selected. Our own facial expression was the only index to her; and even if we had not purposely looked as neutral as possible, it is difficult to imagine how we could have consciously carried, say, the two of diamonds written on our foreheads.

The powers of the Creery sisters began to wane after 1882, however, and further experiments were carried out with two young men from Brighton, G.A. Smith and Douglas Blackburn; the latter was a journalist and the former a hypnotist, and significant results were obtained. Alas, in *The Daily News* of 1 September 1911, after the deaths of Podmore, Gurney and Myers, Blackburn looked back with sorrow on duplicity:

> I, with mingled feelings of regret and satisfaction, now declare that the whole of these alleged experiments were bogus, and originated in the honest desire of two youths to show how easily men of scientific mind and training could be deceived when seeking for evidence in support of a theory they were wishful to establish.

But can Blackburn's revelations, thirty years after the events, be taken as unblemished truth?

Time and again, particularly in the case of mediums, sustained experimental work reveals inconsistencies of behaviour: on one occasion a sensitive may reveal telepathic or extra-sensory powers, while on another fraud may be practised by the same individual. This, perhaps, may be equated with our everyday behaviour, where we are tempted to embellish our experiences with dramatic licence here and there; it is as if the excitement of a novel or a play needs to be extended occasionally into our reports and conversations.

Meticulous recordings of the Smith/Blackburn experiments, consisting of transmitting drawings, physical sensations, numbers, words and colours, are to be found in the first volume of *SPR Proceedings* for 1882/3. In the first experiments on 3 December 1882, where Smith was blindfolded with his back to the experimenters, and Blackburn faced them holding Smith's hands, they may well have resorted to some complex code of hand pressures. Colours, pains inflicted on Blackburn (e.g. on the lobe of his right ear) and names (Wissenschaft repeated as Wissie, Wissenaft) were guessed at well beyond chance level. Drawings were also transmitted in this manner. Of further experiments, from the 19th to the 24th January, 1883, in which 37 drawings were transmitted, 29 were successful. Perhaps the most crucial comment, made jointly by Barrett, Gurney, Myers and Podmore, is in Vol. 1 of the *SPR Proceedings*, 1883:

> Let our readers who may be familiar with the morse or any other code of signals, try in some way to convey a description of some of our drawings, to a friend who is blindfolded and has not seen the original . . . the material for possible signs appears to be reduced to shuffling on the carpet, coughing and modes of breathing. Anything distinctly unusual in any of these directions must inevitably have been noticed . . .

A crucial report, one concerning drawings, not only gives significant results, but also shows to what extreme measures our early pioneers were driven in order to demonstrate the rigour of their methods:

> However, with the view of removing all doubts that may arise as to possible auditory communications, we on one occasion stopped Mr. Smith's ears with putty, then tied a bandage over his eyes and ears, then fastened a bolster-case over his head, and over all threw a blanket which enveloped his entire head and trunk. Fig. 22 was now drawn by one of us, and shewn outside the room to Mr. Blackburn, who on his return sat behind Mr. Smith, and in no contact with him whatever, and as perfectly still as it is possible for a human being to sit who is not concentrating his attention on keeping motionless to the exclusion of every other object. In a few minutes Mr Smith took up the pencil and gave the successive reproductions shewn below.

So it is that a hundred years later we must balance such an account against the newspaper confession of Blackburn. A return is made to these experiments at a later point in this book, where the matter of drawings transmitted by extra-sensory means emerges as perhaps more common than was thought to be the case in 1883.

In summary, early researchers advanced knowledge on the subject of telepathy by collecting data which yet generally awaits patient scrutiny and classification. The scholars were better at collecting case histories than the scientists, who in turn were more imaginative in generating theories as to how telepathy might work. William Crookes focussed on the action of the brain, notably in terms of electrical activity, and upon thought; Barrett drew attention to ideas and emotions being transmitted; and the rather unorthodox Wallace robustly opposed the ideas of Gurney and Myers that subliminal consciousness was the means of communication, and suggested that discarnate influence facilitated telepathic transmission. Lodge imagined telepathy to be outside physical and temporal means of communication.

Canon Charles Kingsley, creator of *The Water Babies*, suggested that DoAsYouWouldBeDoneBy is no bad basis for social harmony. Applying this to investigators and producers of psychic data, it seems that the former have often displayed less than courteous goodwill to the latter. Indeed, Messrs. Hall and Slater in 1980 were pitiless in their criticisms of the long-dead Myers, Podmore and Gurney, and general attitudes towards mediums, telepathists, hypnotists have not been dissimilar over the past century.

The question might thus be asked, 'Who has the *right* to pronounce judgement?' In the matter of the activities of physicists and lawyers, say, the answer is simple: professional groups should be judged by their peers, who equal them in knowledge and, importantly, public prestige. But everybody is a parapsychologist of sorts and most feel qualified to judge both morally and from the angle of appropriate knowledge backgrounds; hence, in the past, pioneers in this field have always had to go, almost cap in hand, to a heterogeneous selection of bodies and individuals to seek approval, from physical scientists via Church leaders to the general public. (This last named, of course, has always been influenced by the socially prestigious and eminent.)

One of the main reasons why the early researchers were often almost condemned to oblivion was that they failed to approach sympathisers or even neutrals for validation; and often they were almost obsequious in not questioning the right to do so of

Pioneers of thought transference studies
Edmund Gurney (1847–1888) and Henry Sidgwick (1838–1900)
were founder members of the SPR and saw telepathy as
demonstrating spirituality in human nature

those who probed at their methods, data and methodologies. Yet when the SPR investigated the Theosophical Society in 1887, courtesy and moderation prevailed in the reported investigation, even though the critical conclusions were later ridiculed by Madame Blavatsky, leader and founder of the movement. Let us hope that such civilized modes of investigation will apply to future research examinations in telepathy.

It may be of passing interest to note that a majority of our researchers were the sons of clergymen and must have been relentlessly exposed to Church ritual and dogma in their formative years, later to reject such orthodoxies. From such conventional perspectives they moved on to agnosticism and then parapsychology, and strongly felt the need to demonstrate that there was an important non-material element to humans which might well survive death. Telepathy was seen as something of a signpost to this belief.

We should now pass on to more detailed accounts of telepathic exchanges, as experienced by different individuals and social groups at various places and times.

PART TWO

Experiences

1

Among primitive societies

In his little-known autobiography entitled *Magical Mission*
published in 1954, George Sandwith, aristocratic explorer, land
agent, soldier and sensitive, sums up prevailing differences
between our own and so-called primitive societies after recount-
ing one of the many psychic traveller's tales in his book:

> Laugh it off if you like. But I believe that there are enormous
> possibilities that we in the West have overlooked in our hurry
> to grab as much wealth as possible in the shortest possible
> time.

For it is a matter of interminable debate whether primitive
socieites are so undeveloped in terms of links with basic and
hidden forms of nature – and in human relationships. In
sociological jargon, expressive bonds are stronger between
closely knit groups than in our urban culture where instrumental, role-related behaviours are more common. It was,
perhaps, left to Dan Leno to simplify such concepts and sum up
the tension between warmth and practicality when he
commented:

> London is a large village on the Thames where the principal
> industries carried on are music halls and the confidence trick.

At once the matter arises as to what can be quoted as evidence
of telepathic experiences in non-industrialised societies, for a
certain amount of direct quoting from texts become necessary,
as in many other parts of such a book as this. The reality of any
telepathic experience is passed, and perhaps refracted, through
several filters: from the original event; to the native's account;

the traveller's recollection and recording of the event; the publisher's screening of the traveller's tale in print; my selective perception of the writer's words; and lastly (mercifully) my abstracted account to be passed on to your perceptions and habits of thought. Such a massive sentence savours of the lugubrious and obvious, but it is a necessary preliminary to a selection of accounts of telepathic experiences in primitive societies. It is only when independent evidence accumulates and begins to form a pattern of some kind – and even patterns are, of course, socially constructed – that the variables of sequential accounts become dissolved into probabilities.

I have limited my selections to writers who strike me as being generally honest and whose records are also typical of many other accounts which I have read through the years. All are, in my view, fair minded, imaginative and sympathetic to those about whom they write; they also attempted on their travels to empathize with the native cultures in which they found themselves and with the experiences of those giving accounts in terms unfamiliar to most of us. Lastly and most importantly, I suppose I quote from them because their ideas and style of presentation appeal to me.

Sandwith was born into the aristocracy and knew the rigours of a public-school education where he met with mixed fortunes, progressing from rebel to house prefect. After a spell as a tobacco planter he joined the Army at the outbreak of the Second World War and found himself in Ethiopia, where he was given an ikon and his psychic self became aroused. He describes the experience thus:

Whenever I looked at the Ikon for about twenty minutes, preferably in a dim light, a voice spoke to me (as it were, inside myself). On the first occasion the voice told me that if I should ever part from the Ikon during my lifetime I would have the most appalling bad luck . . . on the second occasion it told me that I must give up the impersonal type of meditation that I tried to carry out once a day – for such a path was not for me. What I required was something warm and emotional, and that could be obtained by meditation on the Ikon. After a while it seemed natural to go to the Ikon whenever I felt worried or perplexed; a warm soothing feeling would spread through my mind and body, radiating out from the navel, and after this I found I could relax naturally. Most problems are easy to solve while one is relaxed and happy, and on the other hand worry and nervous tension are bad companions.

This theme of moving from the ordinary, conscious level to a deeper and more relaxed state, in which subliminal parts of the mind may operate, is one which occurs time and time again in accounts of influencing others at a distance. In primitive societies such a state may be achieved by rhythmic dancing or, as Richard St. Barbe Baker, another traveller in Africa (see page 48) emphasizes, by drumbeats, so that the everyday perceptions are stilled and muted and other extra-sensory perceptions may be aroused.

Sandwith deals with dowsing, fire walking and curses in his book, and describes at one point how white Kenya farmers suffered no ill-effects when cursed at a distance by African wizards, for, he believes, their Western upbringing had brought about no subconscious conditioning which might have made them susceptible to psychic attackers. However, while in Fiji, both his treasured ikon and a mummified sacred cuttlefish given to him while in Tonga were both needed to counter a similar attack made on him. He had been posted to a Fijian village during the war on government business, and had met with much hostility. One of the witches in the village ('an enormous woman with a hooked nose and little piggy eyes') was deputed to deal with him.

> I sat down in a deck-chair inside the Rest House to read a book, when something made me look up – and there was this horrible giantess whom I had met in the road, staring at me through the French windows. For a moment I held those devil's eyes with my own, and then she looked down, and went off to have a long talk with the housekeeper in the kitchen.

At nightfall the attacks became intensified, the housekeeper taking away the pressure lamp and leaving Sandwith with only a weak oil lamp. Upon praying, he was told to place his ikon under his pillow and the cuttlefish under his legs.

The witch who had watched me through the French windows had fastened shadowy cords on to my stomach and she was busy sucking life force out of my body and pumping fear back, on the principles of black magic, common to all ages. I knew what to do, and symbolically severed the cords, when I immediately felt a release. In spite of this the deadly chill soon returned, so I went to bed and turned out the oil lamp, after putting the Ikon under my pillow and the Cuttlefish under my legs, as directed.

So his struggle continued, with Fijians partolling outside directing torch beams on to his bed from time to time. The attacks by cold rays continued, but gradually he overcame them.

After a while warmth flooded my whole body, so that my stomach felt as if a hot plaster had been put over it, though the heat was internal. This beautiful warmth prepared me for anything.

No doubt sceptics might point to natural drops in temperature in Fiji, or query the evening drinking habits of Sandwith. However, he goes on to describe other hostile psychic encounters in Fiji, and concludes that these involved some sort of intuitive dislike of the Tongan cuttlefish as much as his British origins. But at least he extends his traveller's tale beyond the mere level of narration, and attempts some sort of analysis, however far-fetched it may seem to many.

Travellers who have visited primitive societies are generally agreed as to the emphasis placed there upon the clan or tribe as opposed to the individual. In cultures based on hunting or agriculture working with others against harsh nature is imperative to survival; so it is that family ties at both nuclear and extended levels are of prime importance and there are deep emotional links between relatives, blood brothers – or whatever the designation may be. There are also the obvious common physical characteristics between families.

One of the more widespread Western beliefs associated with such tribes is that the killing of one's enemies may be effected at a distance, often without the person involved being aware of the dire intentions of the evil wisher. Ideas of pins being stuck into images, threads twisted around miniature throats, or mere hating in the appropriate direction are commonplace and, of course, much lurid fiction abounds on the subject.

Is there any truth in such accounts? Can the predatory fasten in this way on to the unsuspecting? Might not these phenomena be applied to Western situations in spite of the convictions of George Sandwith? These questions legitimately raise themselves in such a book as this, for the very nature of the telepathic process may be at the heart of such bizarre interchanges.

First, stories of killing at a distance abound in many cultures, particularly in the West Indian Island of Haiti, the Hawaiian Islands, Malaya and Africa. Witch doctors are commonly involved in such practices, and are thought to generate the necessary malignant psychic influence. A doctor who had spent most of his working life in Kenya is quoted by J.C. Barker in his book *Scared to Death* as saying:

> I am perfectly convinced that Africans can die of their own free will, that they can die literally of fear and that in some way spells cast by witch-doctors can bring about the deaths of those who have been bewitched.

An instance is given of a head dresser he knew in an African hospital who had been told that the witch doctor of a tribe had bewitched him and who felt his strength ebbing away from day to day. However, his friends were able to discover a bundle of sticks, leaves, nail clippings, hair and a tooth from the victim, which were hanging above the entrance to the hut where he lived in his tribe. The witch doctor was prevailed upon to remove the spell and the victim made a recovery. Obviously auto-suggestion played a big part, but there are dozens of cases where the victim has no knowledge of the bewitchment but perishes for apparently unaccountable reasons. The whole area, of course, awaits systematic collection and analyses of data, to strike a prosaic parapsychological note, which is often strangely at variance with the atmosphere of such accounts.

What seems likely from case histories is that Western men and women, lacking tribal links and socialization into such a process, seem unaffected by remote malevolencies. One can easily imagine, for example, the ill-will engendered by ruthless bureaucrats or tycoons on their upwardly mobile journeys: those ground into bankruptcy by the railway barons, the victims of Hitler, generations of suffering schoolchildren – all these potential wishers of ill to their tyrants have seemingly had little effect in any attempts at psychic retaliation. Death by distant thinking thus seems much associated with tribal rituals and inner feelings of inevitable death if certain processes or symbols are employed; urban man appears to be more or less immune.

A very real difficulty in selecting travellers' tales from distant parts is that of sheer volume; many are the explorers and others who have spent parts of their lives abroad, and many are the memoirs, often unconsciously exaggerated or self-glorified. To find any nuggets relating to telepathic experiences – let alone tentative explanations – is not easy.I have thus elected to concentrate finally on but two writers – Laurence Van der Post and Richard St. Barbe Baker. I feel that these two men both empathized well with those among whom they lived for long periods and managed to obtain insights into telepathic processes better than most.

Here are three accounts from Van der Post, writing of the Bushmen in the Kalahari Desert.

Once Van der Post was told by an old Bushman that people were coming. He graphically describes standing in the hot sun with a few others, with silence all around except 'the day roaring like a furnace' in his ears. His conversation with an old interpreter ran as follows:

'Are you sure there are people coming this way?'
'Oh yes! I feel them coming here!' He tapped a finger on the smooth yellow skin of his bare chest.
'Men and women in trouble coming this way.'

Such proved to be the case a few minutes later. A small group of men, women and children appeared, thirst-racked and starving, having been separated from their tribe during famine conditions. They were given food and water, and Van der Post stated that there was not a grown-up person who 'drank less than a gallon'.

Some occult signals of distress had made themselves known to the old native, and telepathy theory is again at a sad loss to shed any light on the matter. Clearly the signals were felt by the interpreter, but whether they moved from a distance into the senses of the old man, or whether he experienced simultaneous feelings of distress cannot be deduced. Again, it seems that we must break fresh conceptual ground in search of an explanation, perhaps involving the physical, emotional and psychic make-up of both the agents and the percipient. It is of interest, perhaps, that the interpreter was presumably trying to pick up distress signals of some kind, thus perhaps sensitising that part of him, visible or invisible, which allowed of such a process.

A further case from Van der Post refers to what he calls the telegraphy in the spirit of the Bushman, which one described thus:

> The Bushmen's letters are not in their bodies. The letters speak, they move, they make the Bushmen's bodies move. The Bushmen order the others to be silent: a man is altogether silent when he feels his body is tapping inside.

This tapping serves to indicate safe ways to go, and also (to most of us incredibly) indicates not only the proximity of animals outside sensory range, but also how creatures may be feeling or even what they are doing. 'Only those who are stupid and do not understand these teachings disobey the tappings in themselves,' one Bushman observed.

Van der Post echoes these ideas and suggests that we reduce our 'clamour of words' so that we, modern man, might again hear 'his rejected aboriginal self, his love of life and element of renewal, tapping on his own back door'.

The third incident is taken from one specific example among several. Van der Post instances a Bushman who not only knew that an ostrich was approaching, even though not within sight, but also that it was scratching the back of its neck with its foot. He deduced or rather empathized this since he experienced a tapping in his own neck at the same place where the ostrich was scratching. This is, of course, unprovable and a wild humorist might fantasize as to serious-faced researchers from the SPR carrying out controlled experiments at a distance involving ostriches, percipients, telephones, recorders and much else. It is only by reading similar accounts from travellers at different times and places that the general feature of Africans being able to sense animals at a distance, by referring to states in their own bodies, may be fairly deduced. 'I know the zebra is near for I feel his stripes on my back' was a response from an African friend of my acquaintance when he was discerning telepathy. Again, the somewhat prosiac business of collecting accounts to discern patterns awaits eager researchers.

One significant writer on Africa whose book *Africa Drums* (now long since out of print, alas) repays close study is Richard St. Barbe Baker who was a conservator of forests in Kenya and Nigeria earlier this century. He spent much of his life with natives and his adventures and opinions are prefaced by Bronislaw Malinowski, some time sociologist at London University, enormously popular lecturer, and controversial figure generally. Malinowski was a great believer in participant observation, or living for long periods with groups in order to understand cultural features; and after an account of a long spell with Trobriand Islanders had been duly published (with Malinowski renamed 'Man of Songs' by the natives) one critic remarked that it was remarkable how strong a resemblance the ebullient characteristics of the Trobriand Islanders bore to those of Professor Malinowski.

True or false, the jibe is worth considering. In *Africa Drums* St. Barbe Baker is perhaps exhibiting his adventurous nature when he writes:

> Oh would that I were a young man again but with all the knowledge that Africa has given me, to start where I left off and once more travel by night along the star-roofed Jamieson River between the aisles of mighty trees; like the African, ignore the divisions of time, and with him practice those faculties now lost to us, but which he has retained.

But even allowing for undue subjectivity of approach (all would not find Africa so enchanting), there is the suggestion that non-industrialised countries have atmospheres which facilitate an appreciation of nature and, in consequence, a greater development of the more sensitive sides of our natures, of which telepathy is one manifestation.

Africa Drums may well serve as a useful primer for those who would study the mystery of telepathy. In it are first-hand accounts of telepathy (or 'television' as St. Barbe Baker chooses to call it) and also much interesting theory. He draws attention to the importance of drums not only in arousing 'sensual community' for appropriate ceremonial occasions, but also in generating some subtle rhythm in response to which events may be perceived at a distance. Among several incidents mentioned in his book the following is typical and carries with it interesting speculations, in SPR terms, of etheric, subconscious or auric explanations. Certainly the psychic energy field surrounding humans seems to be well recognised by Africans, as does the Mesmeric idea of some great, timeless, joining atmosphere. A first step, of course, is to generate commonly acceptable terms which would facilitate discussion and research, and Baker's account and the language of expression reflects the present difficulties experienced in describing such incidents. He sets the scene thus:

> One day at noon I pitched my tent as near as possible to the imaginary line known as the Equator where it passes through the foothills of Mount Kenya . . . the sky was a pure azure, the air fresh, and the sun not unpleasantly hot. It was one of those days which are not infrequent on the Equator at an elevation of six thousand feet. . . .
>
> Lunch was served by a boy, who observed that Bwana Katchiku had died, this man being a well-respected farmer who lived some two hundred and fifty miles from the camp. When asked how he knew, the boy replied that N'degwa, one of the elders of the tribe about sixty years old, had 'seen' it. He sent for the older man, who saluted as they shook hands.
>
> 'What is this? Bwana Katchiku dead, do you say? How did you learn of this?'
>
> 'N'iona, I see it,' was his astonishing answer.
>
> 'When?' I demanded.
>
> 'Now,' he said. Somehow I knew he was speaking the truth, nor was there any reason for him to do otherwise.
>
> 'I am sorry,' I told him. 'It is too bad Bwana Katchiku was a good master'.

Talking drums
St. Barbe Baker
believed that rhythms
and sounds generated
by East African
drums such as those
shown here served as
psychic wavelengths
for transmitting
information over
hundreds of miles

'Yes that is so,' agreed N'degwa. 'It is a bad business'.

N'degwa retired, but I made a mental note of the time and place. I pondered on the word N'iona – I see – which could not possibly be confounded with S'kia – I hear.

Seven days later a runner arrived at my camp with the news that Bwana Katchiku had died, at a distance of two hundred and fifty miles from camp.

No doubt instances from African and other so-called uncivilized societies could be added interminably from various travellers' tales coloured or not by personal bias and refracted through recollection. What is significant in Baker's book is that he advances some sort of mechanism for what he calls 'television' – literally seeing at a distance. This, of course, is what we do not do when we regard a television screen: we are looking at a collection of varying light intensities on a cathode ray tube a few feet away. Baker bases his explanation on drums. He writes:

> They are shrouded in mystery as the very atmosphere. Atmosphere is the word that springs to mind. May it not be that drums create the atmosphere for the transmission of thought messages and vision which annihilate time and space? The more deeply I have delved into the problem of transmission, the more I have become convinced of the inseparable association between the transmission of a visual picture by telepathic means and the language of the drum. . . .

Here might one synthesize, a little daringly perhaps, and point to the rapport between hypnotist and subject, between clairvoyant and those sitting in a circle, and the stage performer and his telepathic act, code or no. There is the same concentration brought about as in the case of the African drum, the same blending of human and etheric atmospheres, to use the terminology available. It is when this stage of mental assonance is achieved that communication between agent and percipient may take place. The tuning forks are identical, as it were, and when one is struck the other resonates.

Certainly non-industrial societies, from both the far past and the near present, afford great opportunities for the telepathy researcher. There is the possibility for gathering data, which is undeniable (such as deaths at great distance), and of considering subjective reports of percipients. Such ideas as 'tapping' or 'drums' or 'rhythm' may well be at least detailed.

The bizarre matter of messages coming from the future, using the intermediary of drum rhythm, is suggested by a last traveller's tale from Baker's book:

> I had a headman called N'duma. For my entertainment he had arranged for an evening with the drums. Two young men, or morans, incessantly played on their drums for about a couple of hours until even I became almost hypnotized with the monotony. Suddenly N'duma explained.
>
> 'Master, I see you are going for a journey. You are going up to my country. You are going to Meru.'
>
> At that time I had no intention of going to Meru. It was out of my district and there was, as far as I knew, absolutely nothing to take me there.
>
> 'What makes you say that, N'duma?' I asked.
>
> 'N'iona', was the reply, meaning simply, 'I see it.'

A week later, the forester was duly informed that he should go two hundred miles away to Meru, on an unexpected mission and, as he notes, it is difficult to conceive how his approaching journey could have been 'televised' a week before it took place. Thus are we back at the realization that telepathic messages, as with clairvoyance, may be, as we term it, past present or future.

As we move towards the end of the twentieth century, we become increasingly aware that urbanization has been over-valued in human terms. The many movements for conservation of resources, the realizations that our past rural history should be accurately and sympathetically recorded and, above all perhaps, that Third World countries have much to offer at higher cultural levels – all these are indicators of our growing (or grown) disenchantment with industrial society.

Let us leave the last word to St. Barbe Baker, writing of London in the 1930s:

> I shall never forget what a shock it was to me, when after a long tour of services in Africa, returning to London I rode on

a bus along Oxford Street and looked down on what seemed to me, by comparison with the remembrance of magnificent bodies, such puny little people with short, shuffling steps, hurrying to and fro, jostling each other, all intent on catching buses or peering through plate-glass windows at thousands of things I couldn't imagine anyone needing. The rhythm of life was conspicuous by its absence – no song or dance, but an air of worry and anxiety in competition in the weekly rush for the bargain basement. How different from the serenity of the forest or wayside market!

2

In wartime

It is said that the First World War midwifed intelligence-testing and widespread secondary education: hitherto unequalled opportunities for measuring men *en masse* at physical and mental levels presented themselves and social consciences were accordingly aroused. Similarly, and even more poignantly, links of love and comradeship were tested as perhaps never before or since, and psychic consequences concerning the sustenance or rupture of such bonds were recorded more readily. As yet, in human studies, few serious attempts have been made either to collate or to reason on from such heartfelt accounts; the field of telepathic communication has, however, been enriched by the many descriptions of transmitted thoughts, feelings and actual bodily appearances at death.

Reports of telepathy were on a far wider scale, at an extra-sensory level, than is imagined at the present time but few went to the extent of recording messages, feelings or appearances and word-of-mouth accounts. These went the way of many other salient historical references; for history, at least until the advent of radio and television, has largely been written history; the voice of the working-man in the nineteenth century, for example, is rarely available, together with all the finer shades of social and human meaning that it might have brought us today.

Two books which include several cases reported verbally are *Psychic Phenomena and the War* by Hereward Carrington and *Ghosts in the Great War*, this latter being a collection of recollections of *Daily News* readers. There are other even more detailed descriptions of the life beyond, as in *Raymond* by the son of Sir Oliver Lodge, or *Gone West* by J.S.M. Ward, or *The Country Beyond* by Jane Sherwood. These make comforting reading but, somehow, it all seems rather too good to be true. ('Come let us sit down beside this fountain and discuss the matter', said the young officer.) Such works are interesting, but do not fall within the aims of this chapter which considers transmissions between living and living, or living and dead, in wartime situations and looks for patterns.

Hereward Carrington was a distinguished student of psychical research. He had been actively engaged with Professor Hyslop, a leading American parapsychologist and formerly Professor of Ethics and Logic at Columbia University, at the end of the nineteenth century and had reported on a series of sittings with the notable Italian medium Eusapia Palladino in 1909. In *Psychic Phenomena and the War* he writes feelingly of those fighting for the allied cause, which he equates with justice, truth and humanism, and with scorn of the Germans, whom he links with materialism and bestial atrocities – in the early part of the book he spares no reader the details of inhuman behaviour, towards both military and civilian personnel. In later chapters, he cites cases involving telepathic bonds between agents and percipients. This involves a desire on the part of the agent either to be with the percipient or transmit a message of some kind, and certainly the space between the parties is bridged; the times of contact mostly conjoin, so that, for example, a soldier going into a dawn attack at 6.30 and being mortally wounded within minutes appears to the percipient at that time. Here are two accounts taken at random:

> It was during the great war, my fiancé was a soldier in the Army of the Rhine – if I do not mistake – and for a long time we had no news of him. During the night of the 23rd of August I had a singular dream which tormented me, but to which I did not attach much importance. I found myself in a hospital ward, in the midst of which was a kind of table on which my fiancé was lying. His right arm was bare and a severe wound could be seen near the right shoulder; two physicians, a Sister of Charity, and myself were near him. All at once he looked at me with his large eyes and said to me, 'Do you still love me?' The soldier died at that time and with a Sister of Charity in attendance.

There is a popular belief that between twins there exists at times an affinity which surpasses the normal . . . a certain corporal, who was with his regiment at a home station, had been anxious for some time about his twin brother who was fighting in France. He had not heard from him for some weeks, and as he had been a fairly regular correspondent, this worried him a great deal.

One night he was awakened from a deep sleep by the sound of his name being spoken; he sat up in bed and listened, but the call was not repeated. And then, as he looked across the room, in the semi-darkness he saw quite plainly his brother sitting on his trunk, which was near the door.

The twin brother had been wounded at the Battle of Loos at the very hour when he had seemed to see him sitting on the box in his room.

It may be worth noting at this point that the wounded are discreet about their injuries; when one considers the appalling mutilations sustained under trench warfare it seems slightly odd that wounds should either be superficial (in terms of, say, blood on the forehead or apparently intact torsos) or that the whole and often uniformed body of the agent presents itself. It was, oddly, the lot of a fiction writer, W.W. Jacobs, to suggest the horror of visitations by the mutilated dead in his story *The Monkey's Paw*.

These twin themes of benevolent corporal wholeness or minimal signs of wounding are generally borne out in the accounts of readers of *The Daily News* who had telepathic experience from dead or wounded near and dear. It could be, of course, that agents wanted to spare the feelings of percipients as much as possible: the need was there to communicate, and the loved one at home was given a mental picture of some acceptable actuality. Consider, for example, these three readers' accounts from the collection of telepathic episodes:

In August of 1917 my brother was fighting in France for his King and country. One Sunday night I had gone to bed and just turned out the light and made a prayer for the safe keeping of my brother who was fighting for us, when he appeared before me, bent over me and gave a lovely smile and disappeared again. Two days afterwards I received a letter to say he was killed in action at the hour he appeared to me.

One day during the war, I was sitting reading, when suddenly I heard my fiancé (then in France) calling my name. I looked up and beheld him walking towards me, in a white shroud. I was horrified and called to him to go away, but his ice cold hands touched my face and I fainted. He was killed that day and his comrades said he was calling my name as he died . . .

My mother went to bed in a worried state . . . waking up at midnight she saw Will leaning over the bed-rail in his uniform, with his head in bandages. She called him by name and he came towards her but, when she put out her hand to touch him, he vanished. News soon came that Will died on that same midnight from head wounds. (The mother had retired to bed in a state of anxiety as a robin had hopped through the house that day. On the three other occasions, when each of her other three sons had been killed, a robin had hopped through her house.)

Here indeed, we seem to be getting into deeper water than our present-day paradigms would comfortably allow us to wallow in. As was mentioned in the hundreds of cases collected in *Phantasms of the Living* by Gurney, it is quite possible for people to experience phantasms of those close to them who have died. The war cases merely confirm Gurney's ideas and the power of ties of affection to facilitate such visitations. But what of the robin hopping through the house? If it is accepted as true (and it would be a remarkably unusual yarn to spin) then perhaps there is a whole odd territory of ominous behaviours to chart, including all manner of signs and symbols. However, this book is concerned with telepathy, its incidence and possible mechanisms, and a passing reference to such mysteries is all that is called for.

These accounts reveal a very important clue on our telepathic trail; that where there is heightened emotional activity, perhaps arising from physical injury or fear, then possibilities of telepathic transmissions are enhanced.

Why is this? Some French writers suggest that the subconscious mind operates more effectively when the emotions are excited and the conscious mind reduced in operational power and efficiency; other ideas are that the nerve aura is more extensive under an increased blood flow, thus helping telepathic powers, or that the autonomic nervous system comes into more intense operation and this, also, has links with the subconscious mind. Besides increased states of physical and emotional anguish, such as are commonplace on the battlefield, there is the matter of kin relationships. This also means a commonality of physique and other genetic similarities, which may also mean a resemblance of nervous systems. Between identical twins, in particular, there is often a great rapport and many reported telepathic experiences.

The following case from the Second World War is interesting in that it illustrates heightened emotional states, kin and affection relationships, and also a real desire on the part of one party to *receive* a communication which might mean the difference between life or death. It is taken from McKenzie's book, *Apparitions and Ghosts*, a classical work which was three years in the making and is endorsed by the eminent philosopher H.H. Price.

The woman involved (she was a schoolgirl in 1943) described a lunchtime raid on the school buildings.

> Then someone shouted 'They're Jerries!' so we ran for the nearest reinforced classroom. I was just inside the doorway when a bomb hit the school, demolishing two thirds of the building.
>
> For some seconds it was silent (or I went deaf). Then there were deafening screams, as it was pitch black and our mouths full of grit and dust. We just stood petrified, screaming.
>
> Suddenly, to my left, I saw a ray of light and my father stood there, and I said 'Oh Dad, Help us'. He just smiled and beckoned so I called out, 'Come on, it's my Dad – this way'. We went towards the light and found a space in the debris out into the playground.
>
> About two hours later, arriving home, I was surprised to find mother there because she normally didn't get home until five. She said, 'A policeman came to the works to tell me Dad died this morning at 8 o'clock, so they let me come home'.

A point of further interest is that her father appeared to be wearing 'a collarless shirt with the top button undone, and trousers, just as he used to be dressed when relaxing after work before he was ill . . .' A recurring and intriguing feature in the appearance of apparitions is the significance of clothes; does the discarnate entity select them or is the percipient the determining factor? A further significant statement crops up when the girl reached home '. . . I was rather comforted in the knowledge that he had come to help me but at the same time I didn't tell anyone in case they thought I was mad.' Even after twenty-five years she hadn't told her mother and, apart from communicating by letter with McKenzie as to the incident, had told only her husband. The amount of raw data on this subject may thus be more universal then is generally supposed.

Here is more evidence that in times of danger and stress, with a heightening of the emotions, a muting of the mental, and a possible amplification of subconscious features, that some strong message goes forth to the living as well as discarnate loved ones. John Barrymore, outstanding actor and doomed alcoholic from the Twenties, experienced a similar helpful appearance from a loved one when he was in a state of some fear and desperation. He had been stalking game birds and had sunk up to his waist in a quagmire. Gene Fowler, in his biography of the actor, relates Barrymore's account:

> Now I distinctly saw my dead father's face rising before me. I could envision him as clearly as ever I had seen him in my boyhood. I had been getting desperately numb and full of futility until I saw my father's face. He turned his eyes towards an overhanging scrub which, in the surprising suddenness of everything I had not noticed until now. With great effort I managed to draw a branch within reach of my fingers, using the stock of my gun as 'fetcher'.

After a desperate five-minute struggle Barrymore managed to extricate himself; of all people, he could be dubbed a romantic witness but, for me anyway, there is a certain sincerity to the account.

One case quoted by Robert Dale Owen, in his book *Footfalls on the Boundary of Another World*, concerning the death of a Captain Wheatcroft at Lucknow in 1857, is interesting in that it endorses the link between the time of death and the appearance of an apparition, and also that the latter may appear to more than one person. ('Apparition' usually refers to a spectral form which appears only once or twice and for the purposes of passing on some kind of information. 'Ghost' refers to one which appears repeatedly and, by comparison, rather aimlessly.) The soldier had been killed on the afternoon of 14 November and his apparition appeared about nine in the evening to a friend of the Wheatcroft family's solicitor who was a medium. During the night Mrs. Wheatcroft awoke and saw the figure of her husband in uniform, with his hands pressed to his chest. She said that she saw him 'as distinctly as she had ever done in her life'. The figure remained visible for about a minute and then disappeared. A telegram later arrived saying that he had been killed before Lucknow on 15 November. The wife, unsurprised by the news, queried the date and later, early in 1858, received a certificate from the War Office confirming the date. However, in March the Wheatcroft family received a letter from a fellow officer who stated that he had been close to the slain soldier when he died on the afternoon of 14 November. He had been struck in the breast by a fragment of a shell and buried at Diloosha, with a cross at the head of his grave on which the initials G.W. and the date of his death, 14 November, had been carved. The War Office later amended the date on the certificate.

One well-attested wartime case (it actually occurred in December 1918 but concerned fliers from the war) and reported in *S.P.R. Proceedings*, Vol. xxxiii suggests that there may be coincidence between the exact moment of death and the appearance of an apparition. Pilot David McConnel flew a Camel from Scampton in Lincolnshire to Tadcaster in Yorkshire. After saying that he would be back 'in time for tea' he took off. Lieutenant Larkin had a vision of him at the time of the crash – about 3.20 – and he describes the incident thus:

I heard someone walking up the passage; the door opened with the usual noise and clatter which David always made; I heard his 'Hello, boy!' and I turned half round in my chair and saw him standing in the doorway, half in and half out of the room, holding the doorknob in his hand. He was dressed in full flying clothes, but wearing his naval cap, there being nothing unusual in his appearance. His cap was pushed back on his head and he was smiling, as he always was when he came back into the room and greeted us. I remarked 'Hello, back already?' He replied 'Yes, got there all right, had a good trip '. . . I was looking at him the whole time he was speaking. He said, 'Well cheerio!' closed the door noisily and went out.

McConnel had crashed at Tadcaster at about that time. He had, by some ghostly telepathic process, come back 'in time for tea' to his friend after all. (It may be noted, significantly, that the apparition made reference only to the journey to Tadcaster and *not* the return trip.)

This last case affords a suitable example of how different schools of thought might view unexpected appearances, out of thin air, so to speak, of loved ones and friends. All the points of view have features to recommend them, and a total acceptance of either, or some middling stance, will obviously depend upon individual experience and reading. First, the view of the logicians and materialists: a case could be made for Lt. Larkin, reporter of the incident, having fallen asleep and dreamed the whole thing. The recent departure of his friend, who specifically mentioned that he would be back in time for tea, it may be argued, was in the mind of the man as he nodded off in comfortable surroundings in mid-afternoon. Dreams frequently follow on from matters in the mind, and here is a case in point. The sound of the door being opened noisily and the sight of David wearing the clothes he went out in accord with the kind of detail in dreams which follow recent observations or events. And we all know how very vivid dreams can be. Students of the subconscious might add that there was a hidden anxiety as to the fate of his friend, and a hope that he would get back safely, which led to a dream projection.

Other hard-liners could argue for mis-reporting, exaggeration – or simply mistaken identity. Young fliers must have certain common features of appearance and manner, and there is also the psychological matter of man being the measure of all things and seeing what he wants to see. Misperception and self-delusion are often at the back of many so-called psychic appearances – there are several cases, for example, of moustaches and beards being imagined on the faces of lady mediums who specialize in materializations – the dim lights and shadows often encourage such illusions. After the fashion of the enquiring Gurney, going round his seances in the 1870s, I have sat at the side on the front row at such meetings and have observed no changes, other than contortion of features, while those at the front in the middle have cried out as to hirsute features and associations with near and dear departed. (Should there be an actual change in face structure, this, would of course, be observed in profile as well.)

Those on the side of the angels would say that at death the essence of David McConnel would be subtracted from his physical body; that his astral and mental bodies would rearrange this to represent a materialization solid enough to rattle open a door, bid a cheery message to a friend as to safe arrival, and depart back to some unknown plane *en route* for the next state of his evolution. Here the explanation is outside normal experience, unlike the earlier ones, and hence has only limited acceptance. Much hinges upon the *bona fides* of Lt. Larkin and whether he was in the middle of waking, sleeping or had a hallucinatory experience. (One can more easily now, perhaps, appreciate Frank Podmore's preoccupation in his 1902 book *Modern Spiritualism* with the commonality of hallucinations and his concern that many psychic episodes are misreported – this spirit of scepticism is well maintained today by such men as Hall, Hansel and Milbourne Christopher, the American debunker of fraudulant occult phenomena.)

What, then, might be generalized from cases of visions of the slain or wounded being transmitted to loved ones, close relatives or friends? A first obvious point is that few receive such impressions. Even allowing for the reluctance of people to report instances, and the consequently low incidence of cases being circulated or recorded, it seems that only occasionally is the form of someone killed or wounded sent to appear before percipients. There is no ready explanation for this; it might be argued that where there are very close personal links (between identical twins, mother/child relationships, or bonds between lovers) images are more often transmitted – certainly there seems the necessity for emotional rapport. There are no cases, as far as I have searched, of appearances before people of strangers or remotely connected acquaintances. Bonds of affection are thus capable of linking locations, and although time seems not to be affected a simultaneous transmission and reception seems the rule.

Secondly, the clothes and physical appearance of the suffering person seem to vary: clad in a shroud, uniformed and bandaged, and wearing casual, leisure-wear clothes have been so far quoted. In other, wartime cases uniform seems to be usual, and disturbing injuries seem somehow to be censored by some merciful and invisible source; or perhaps they may be beyond the imagination of civilians at home.

However, two cases in which injury through wounds was visible to the percipient are to be found in a book entitled *One Hundred Cases of Survival after Death* compiled by A.T. Baird and first published in 1943, in the middle of the Second World War. During the war, prevailing conditions seem to have generated a need for literature suggesting that death is not the end, and formidable testimony as to this is given at the front of the book by Messrs. Barret, Lombroso, Geley and Lodge – all very eminent European scientists. Baird draws generously on such classics as Gurney's *Phantasms of the Living* and *SPR Proceedings*.

Case No. 33 concerns the death of Lieutenant Schenck in the war in the Philippines in 1900. He was killed in a Filipino ambush and his sister refers to her mother's reaction thus:

> My mother was sewing one morning at Fort Screven, Georgia, outside Savannah on Tybee Island. She got up from her chair and gave a little cry. It impressed us very much, because she said, 'Oh, I saw your brother. *I saw Will's shoulder disappear* as he fell backwards'.

(The italics are mine.) Here it could be that at the exact moment of death shoulder wounds might have been sustained. But did the lieutenant consciously transmit an image of himself? Or was it the rupturing of the earthly bond which caused it to be sent? Or did the percipient in some telepathic way sense that her son was at the point of death and transcend space in her efforts to be with him?

The other case involving a less than whole appearance is

taken from Gurney's collection, *Phantasms of the Living*. In the East Indian archipelago the Chinese stormed the house of the Rajah of Sarawak, and a Mr. Wellington was beheaded. His sister had a dream at the time when this incident occurred, and her husband described matters thus:

> I was awkened one night by my wife, who was startled from her sleep, terrified by the following dream. She saw her *headless* brother standing at the foot of the bed, with his head lying on a coffin by his side. I did my best to console my wife . . . when the news (of her brother's death) reached England, I computed approximately the time and found it coincided with the memorable night to which I have referred.

A.T. Baird puts forward possible mechanisms by which images may be transmitted by agents to percipients in his hundred cases. It is interesting that the 'old-fashioned' theory to which he refers(see below) has, after the manner of a wheel turning full circle, come more into favour today than he supposes. He writes:

> Do apparitions occupy an objective area in space or are they merely ideas externalized by the percipient's mind? The old-fashioned school favoured the former theory, even though apparitions were seen in unusual clothes. The modern school of psychical research accepts the latter theory, and indeed it is the better explanation of the two; it accounts for the clothes as well. The idea is that the discarnate, more or less successfully, implants by the process of telepathy a certain piece of information concerning himself, and the percipient's mind creates a more or less veridical hallucination.

Baird cannot imagine discarnate thought, or thought emanating from a living person, having the power to project itself through space and assemble itself in corporeal form in clothes of its own choosing. Such a notion, of course, is admittedly very hard to accept. But when considering modern and attested cases of telekinesis (which involves the direction of thought to move material objects), this third possibility emerges with perhaps more credit than Baird supposed. The activities of Uri Geller, Matthew Manning and other telekinetics, together with the production of apports (or solid objects appearing from thin air) at the more worthy of spiritualist seances – all these add weight to the idea of thought being potentially capable of moving through space and affecting material matters.

Wartime experiences thus suggest that during times of sudden bereavement at a distance it is possible for thought impulses to reach others and manifest in bodily form, be it a subjective or objective matter. The sensitivity necessary to receive such impressions seems common to many; rather may it be the intensity of the distant event which facilitates perception.

It is with those who claim to have extra-sensory powers of receiving messages from both the living and the dead that we might next turn in our quest for further telepathic experiences.

[3]

From clairvoyance

Clairvoyants, like plumbers and schoolteachers, vary in ability and performance. At one extreme is the back-street medium, who may charge a few pounds for half an hour of generalizations, gleaned information and a few comforting platitudes revolving around the important matters of love, money and health; at the other end are very gifted sensitives like Eileen Garrett, Estelle Roberts and William King. Their recorded performances before witnesses and in all kinds of situations suggest strongly that some personalities survive death and are able to communicate with those still on earth. Other schools of thought point out that clairvoyants, in both entranced and unworthier professional situations, are adept at telepathy and are able, somehow, to pick up the thoughts of others.

A connection between clairvoyance and telepathy is thus often supposed. Clairaudience is the receiving of messages, in terms of words heard or faces and symbols seen, from those beyond and the transmission of these to members of the audience. Typically, sessions are held at spiritualist churches on Sunday evenings, where there is usually a certain antiseptic brightness about the polished wood lectern, the spruce flower arrangements and the very hearty singing of the more popular hymns. A visiting medium will lead prayers, and perhaps deliver a sermon. She will then pass on to clairaudience.

Some sensitives may take refuge in generalizations when their abilities flag; many would say that these, in essence, are all that is received. What is certain is that the whole matter of clairaudience awaits scrutiny – there is much very rich and provocative data available, and to talk at length with sensitives, as I have done, is to realize that such people are often misjudged. On the whole, there is genuine desire to help, and remuneration is indeed slight, especially in relation to exhaustive journeys up and down the country.

Here are typical examples of messages passed across in scores of spiritualist churches each week:

> Lady in the front row . . . would you understand a recent passing . . . six months ago . . . an accident . . . (respondent says accident was a year ago) . . . gentleman giving the name of William (yes) . . .

> Lady at the end of the row there . . . lady looking like yourself . . . a little fuller in the face and older . . . she brings a warmth . . . a wealth of love and understanding . . . please tell her . . . don't let the grass grow under her feet . . .

> Gentleman at the side here . . . the name Marjorie is called (yes) . . . a George (my father) coming with Arnold (yes) and Sally . . . (yes) . . . she brings you red carnations . . .

> Gentleman over there . . . I get a collie dog . . . sheep farming . . . (yes)

Such messages reveal no surnames, and do not give the sort of information which is passed over the radio on such programmes as requests for records; disc jockeys will rattle off names and addresses and a whole network of family or work connections in a way which makes mediums in clairaudient situations look rather suspect. The general tone seems misty and comforting – the dead rarely seem to be upset, usually appear to good advantage in fine clothes and dwelling in comfortable circumstances . . . in a phrase, it all seems too good to be true. And surely telepathy plays a part somewhere?

It doesn't seem to in many cases. In my interviews with sensitives there is an outspoken honesty which is hard to describe. They all deny any intended or voluntary telepathic communication with recipients, but they do say that scepticism makes no difference; figures and scenes build up around or above members of the audience, and also alongside the medium. Hosts of deceased seem to recognize a channel for communication with audience members. Certainly the trend of present public opinion is against the validity of such performances, and spiritualists claim that they have always had to contend with such prejudice.

Estelle Roberts specialized in clairaudience. In her book, *Some Discern Spirits*, Sylvia Barbanell describes Estelle as being, in the opinion of many, 'the world's greatest medium'. Often as many as 9,000 came to the Albert Hall in London to see and hear her in the wartime years. A few examples of messages will give an idea of the quality of her work; these given below were verified as accurate by recipients:

1. A dead husband, Johnny Dwyer, was correctly described to a wife in the audience and his name given.

2. A man named Russell, who had died in a prison camp in Turkey in the Second World War, brought with him a score of 'the gang' who had also died there in order to communicate with a survivor from the camp in the audience. He gave the names Margetson, Smith, Philpot, Sanders, Rex and nine other surnames – all recognized by the man in the audience.

3. Flt. Lt. 'Cats Eyes' Stevens gave his full name and nickname and, when asked through Estelle Roberts by a fellow flyer Max Whitling how he met his death, he communicated:

   I tried to bale out but my parachute caught in the wing and Jerry brought me down. That's all I know. (This was subsequently confirmed by the Air Ministry.)

4. After giving the name of an air gunner to his wife, '. . . . You spoke to your little girl about some shoes . . . your husband tells me that last week was Baby's birthday; you bought her some shoes and you promised the elder one some on her birthday in April . . . .' The deceased also mentioned incidents which had happened in the home.

5. To the widow of a man killed at Dunkirk: 'Your husband says that last night you spoke aloud. You said 'Buddy, if

you really are on the other side come through tomorrow and prove it. Then I will not doubt any more.' The wife answered that this was true. 'Those were the exact words I used,' she commented.

Another well-known and creditworthy clairvoyant, the aristocratic Geraldine Cummings, was particularly specific as to the qualities of the conscious minds of hopeful sitters, and their capabilities of being influenced by outside spiritual entities. During one sitting she described her spirit control, Astor, in relation to W.B. Yeats who was present and was in the process of preparing a new play at the time but was not consciously thinking about it:

> Astor is an individual separate from myself – being in another world he can read the story in Yeats' subconscious. But he is unable to read the conscious mind of the human being as it belongs to a world that is not his own.

There are many other cases of clairvoyants taking part in what seem to be telepathic processes with clients (a kind of radio-wave between stations seems to be the popular sort of explanation used) when the sensitives themselves would (as in the cases of King, Garrett, Cummings and Roberts) give entirely different explanations of the process and involve guides, dead persons and other spiritual entities. The late Arthur Ford (1902–71) perhaps put the matter most crisply when he wrote of his control, Fletcher, who was instrumental in breaking the famous *post mortem* Houdini code. (The anti-spiritualist illusionist had employed a secret code, known only to his surviving widow, and this Ford communicated to her after the stage magician's death.) He produced much high-quality work with McDougall and others at Duke University in the United States and was once dubbed there as 'the world's greatest medium', echoing Sylvia Barbanell's assessment of Estelle Roberts.

In an interview with *Psychic Magazine* shortly before his death Ford describes the three-way process thus:

> In every sitting with Fletcher, he gets things that the sitter doesn't know, but has to check out. That rules out telepathy

or mind-reading from the sitter. In the early days of my mediumship, most of my sitters were critical investigators, and Fletcher got into the habit of doing this for them. Suppose a grandmother comes and is trying to prove to you who she is. If she gives the name of somebody she knew but that you didn't know, then you have to check it out, and that eliminates the idea of mind-reading.

By contrast, the medium Jeanne Dixon commented, in her interview with the same publication:

> Now then, if I can tune into your channel – which I cannot always do – I can pick up your thoughts and your vibrations, and your purpose upon this earth . . . I use the crystal at times . . . I ask the person to concentrate on one thought only and to look into the crystal. The crystal is my point of concentration. And then I try to pick up his channel, which is his point of concentration, because his thoughts are not scattered. His mind is pointed right there in this beautiful crystal and then I can pick up his thoughts. This is telepathy.

There is probably no simple single causal explanation for telepathy, especially when clairvoyants, who seem to offer different viewpoints, are involved.

Let us now take a look at another clairvoyant – William King, a practitioner in the West End of London who was heavily in demand. He often appeared to read the thoughts of others, and it is interesting to examine his explanations. He was a bespoke tailor, before becoming a leading clairvoyant, whose life is recorded by Charles Drage in the book *William King's Profession* (1960). At a first meeting, the neat and rubicund King took Drage's fountain-pen and gave all manner of details concerning the author's personal life and affairs. This citing of biographical data from holding an object belonging to the subject is usually referred to as 'psychometry' and has a strong link with telepathy, according to some schools of thought: when the object is handled information comes into the mind of the medium which is known to the owner, but not necessarily at a conscious level. Extraneous facts, unappreciated by the subject, may also be added. Here is Drage describing a conversation with King:

Warnings about my numerous enemies, both European and Oriental, took up much of his talk. They were described in meticulous detail and easily indentifiable, often by some unmistakable idiosyncrasy. 'If you say something that displeases him, he'll give you a flashing smile – lots of even, white teeth – and then he'll start to sulk', was one bull's eye. 'Wears a ginger coloured wig, but it's a very good one and you mayn't have noticed: fiddles with a rimless monocle, but never actually puts it up' was another. The monocle I knew well; the wig I spotted the next time I saw it.

Here, clearly and at many other points in the book, is evidence of a very different nature from the generalized comfort given at public sessions. It would be absorbing to consider other of King's target successes, but we are only after anything connected with mental processes and telepathy.

Has he anything to say on mind-reading or processes? Yes he has. And here it may be useful to extend the idea of 'field consciousness', and paraphrase it with a familiar word often used by King – the 'aura' of his client. Within this field, or aura, King can often detect emotional states, as well as see pictures, faces and symbols. Furthermore, extra-sensory visions, sights, sounds and symbols also appear at different points in the room at such sessions, although these are often linked with the aura of his clients. It is as if a spontaneously telepathic process takes place: the medium, King, is able to gain extra-sensory information from the mind of the sitter, even though he or she may not wish to transmit it. And, just to irritate total sceptics, time seems to slide around somewhat: past, present and future events alike are depicted. A few examples from various sittings will serve to describe what King senses and how such telepathic cues link with the realities in the lives of clients:

While figures appear round the client, what I see in front of me are usually *things*, such as houses, motor cars, furniture, jewellery etc. Faces can appear in both positions, but those in front of me are usually only flashes, appearing and disappearing too quickly for me to give the sitter any satisfactory description. Colours appear as in nature, but only if there is sufficient time for them to develop. (Black, writes King, indicates grief or despair, grey boredom or depression while blue, especially light blue, indicates hope or happiness.)

Sometimes, though this is rather rare, half my room will transform itself into some sort of scene. I have glimpsed a graveyard right across my floor and even been able to read the names on the tombstones; but this has only happened three times in thirty years.

The aura can be affected by thoughts and emotions, but only when they are either abnormal or else very violent. Deep and long-lasting depression makes the aura so heavy as to seem almost solid and much the same effect is caused by serious long-lasting anxieties, or alternatively worries which are absolutely insoluble. Lying also has a visible effect though not quite in the same way. When somebody is being untruthful I can see the words coming out of his mouth like breath on a frosty day. The intensity of what I see varies from transparency in the case of 'little white lies' or mildly malicious inventions to something that looks like a heavy fluid when the speaker is being really malevolent.

These are very interesting observations indeed. King is a clairvoyant and thus his senses have a greater range than most, but here we are at the very beginning of an entirely new set of experiences to be measured – for instance, how might one differentiate between 'white lies' and other untrue statements? At the present time of writing the statements of such clairvoyants as King are scattered through biographical pieces and await scrutiny and collection; only then can surmises be made as to whether the thoughts and feelings of people are reflected in their auras. Certainly there is here some evidence that clairvoyants may discern emotional states, and subjects and surroundings known to individuals from their auras or in the vicinity of their auras. This in itself is a hypothesis which has never before been seriously considered and at least merits further investigation.

Again we are back to Wallace's ideas of a discarnate influence, or the dead intervening in communication, if we consider the case of William King's twin brother Joseph. He died at the age of two and, believe it or not, reappeared in bodily form to his living twin brother, for the first time at the age of eight and at intervals through out the life of the medium. When King had progressed into his fifties, Joseph's appearance was still that of a young, healthy-looking man of twenty-five or so, and the medium spoke of the information about a client that he receives from his twin who suggests questions and predicts events. He describes the experience of hearing his twin's voice:

> There are two main differences between his voice and all others. First, whereas other voices seem to come from somewhere inside my head, his comes definitely from outside and sounds exactly as if a living person was whispering close to my ear. Secondly, he seldom speaks unless I am in difficulties – either seeing nothing at all or else hopelessly confused – and have more or less consciously appealed for his help . . . he is a vital factor in my work and without his help I very much doubt if I would be able to work at all.

What seems to be involved in a medium reading the thoughts of others, their feelings and their futures, is the concepts of the human aura and disembodied dead spirits conveying inform-ation between persons. This will seem irritating to many who seek some more prosaic explanation of telepathy, tantamount to taking refuge in some metaphysical Irish bog, and quoting data from the memory of an unknown medium, called William King, to back up such doubtful assertions.

Let us then call on the testimony from one of the most eminent mediums of the twentieth century, Eileen Garrett. She was born in Ireland in County Meath just before the turn of the century and she died in 1970. In her long life she was investigated by many scientific researchers and she herself was interested in putting parapsychology on to some sort of reputable academic footing. To this end she co-operated with nearly all of the leading psychic scientists of her day – Lodge, Doyle, Prince, Rhine, Huxley and Jung were some of the eminent people she worked with.

In an interview with *Psychic Magazine* shortly before her death she reiterated many of her life-long beliefs: that a study of the human aura was vitally important, and that thinking was not confined to the brain – the deepest and most intuitive thinking came, she claimed, from the solar plexus:

I believe that such areas as the solar plexus are where I first sense things, not within the 'thinking' part of my brain. I must get away from objective thinking and allow the subjective areas of the mind to reveal the answer. When this happens, you don't monitor what you're saying, because you're living with an inner voice.

You are looking deep within the self, which I have come to regard as the seat of inspiration. It's all in the region of the solar plexus.

Her psychic experiences, for those unused to reading such accounts, border on the incredible, and critics would no doubt query the accuracy of her reporting. During her life she was, in her own words, able to '*see*, out and beyond physical sight, and *hear* beyond physical hearing'. Such unique capabilities led her to suppose that she was mentally unbalanced, and it was not until the break up of her first marriage during the First World War that she began to make contact with reputable psychic researchers, such as the Swiss Hunli and Hewat McKenzie, and realized that she was a trance medium of unusual power. At many sittings she gave recipients unequivocal evidence of the continued existence of dead friends and relatives. The collection of data *en masse* should help to settle arguments as to validities or qualities of messages, and to what extent a telepathic or spiritualistic explanation might be put forward.

One of her most publicized seances was that held a few days after the death of Conan Doyle in June 1930. It was the hope of the circle that the great man would soon make contact with researchers and perhaps produce a once-and-for-all proof of survival. Mrs. Garrett became entranced and at once began to speak in an agitated voice. Her words purported to come from the dead pilot of the R101, which had crashed at Beauvais in France two days before. She gave half an hour's detailed report of reasons for the airship's crash and freely used aeronautical terms of which she had no conscious knowledge.*

Her philosophy of life, of which what follows is just a part, was

---

* The case has recently been reported in much more acceptable detail in *The Unexplained* Nos. 24 and 25 1981.

clearly expressed in a *Psychic Magazine* interview just before her death:

> You know, we don't just grow up and have misfortunes and difficulties, get the old stuff laid aside, then put a few flowers on the grave and forget about it. That's not life at all. There must be a greater order than we can conceive of – to the whole aspect of being. We have to go, I think, through all kinds of experiences and perhaps after we go, we have to meet another set of circumstances for which we have been prepared or ill-prepared here.

Such a point of view has, of course, been expressed by theologians, poets, philosophers and many other humans through the ages.

Mrs. Garrett preferred to call the aura a 'field' and stated that to her it indicated, better than any other empirical marker, the condition of the body, mind and spirit. These are indeed rather nebulous words, but she points out the need to take account of a person's psychic surround with these words in her auto-biography published in the 1940s:

> I hope that Science will soon become aware of the existence of the *magnetic field* as the diagnostic chart of the state of man's entire being . . . I have described this magnetic field which I see enveloping all human beings, as the receiving station in which man may obtain images, impressions and sensations not only from other people but from many parts of the Universe. These impressions are simultaneously sifted by the response of the mind which accepts or rejects such impressions: They are received and transmitted by a form of radiation which is active throughout nature . . . .

Here, at least, we have a declaration of where thought is registered – within the magnetic field or surround. When she was working at Duke University with Dr. Rhine and his Zener cards (see page 137), she believed that she was working telepathically and not clairvoyantly. She wrote:

> I was able to catch the moving symbols which the mind of

either Dr. Rhine or a student projected to me through space. By being passed through the mind of another, the symbols were thus made to live again and register for me supernormally . . . my interpretation of what takes place, in my own experience, is that the card symbol when thought of, is projected as a light image, moving through space, and thus reaches me as a form of radiation. What I have, since childhood, seen as a nebulous *surround*, enveloping each living organism has, according to my present understanding, a definite use and purpose as receiver and transmitter of radiation through the universe. I have, in recent years, come to call this human aura or surround a *magnetic field*.

Mrs. Garrett also makes a very interesting point about Rhine, which links with the extraordinary successes that he had with Linzmayer and Pearce on occasions, as mentioned in Part Two, Chapter 9. She writes that energy stimulus is necessary to clairvoyance and telepathy and she had 'such a stimulus in my work at Duke, not from the ESP cards, but from the interest and enthusiasm of Dr. Rhine towards the work we were doing. Let me repeat, when he was present, I could produce better results with the ESP cards by taking them telepathically from his mind.'

An interesting corroboration of the ideas of Eileen Garrett is to be found in the autobiography of another medium, Marjorie Staves, in her book *One Step Ahead* (1971). She, too, begins with a sensation in the solar plexus, which she sees as the trigger mechanism for the extension of her senses in the direction of clairvoyance:

The process of picking-up sets off a strange physical tightening in the solar plexus – in the area of the stomach – and not in the head as you might imagine. Ultimately one uses the head, for it is here that the psychic vision or faculty is lodged, but the beginning of contact springs only from the solar plexus. The tension is a little like the sudden sinking grip you feel when you're driving along in the rain and the car skids dangerously. . . . I am projected into another world, a fourth dimension, where I am subjected to heightened sensitivity, instinct, feelings . . .

This sensitive notes that whether she sees subjectively or objectively seems to depend upon her rapport with her client: the aura is all important, and Mrs. Staves maintains that in some strange way knowing the birthday or Zodiac sign of her client may sometimes give additional information at a clairvoyant level.

Some clairvoyants, then, seem to extend their senses of sight and sound beyond the ranges of ordinary people and to pick up pictures and words which seem to come from other dimensions. There are also cases in which the thought process itself may be clairvoyantly perceived within the surround of the person concerned.

In an appendix of *Life Now and Forever* (1942) by Dr. Wills, a past President of the US College of Psychic Science and Research, a remarkable account is given by Wills of how he clairvoyantly observed the mind in action. His story is headed by an anonymous quotation: 'Not one in a million ever gets far enough away from his mind to take a look at it and see the wheels go round.'

First, he projected his etheric from his physical body and was aware of the components of his being: what he calls the 'I' or real self, the mind-field, the psychic body and the physical body. Unfortunately he does not give any visual locations of the first three in relation to the last. Some of his descriptions are interesting: 'The mind aroused desire, which awakened will and set into motion the proper nerve impulses, all distinct and separate in their successive actions.'

But we are not any clearer as to the appearance or process of thought, let alone thought-transference. It is possible that other accounts of the mind in action by clairvoyants might lead beyond everyday ideas, but not without the systematic gathering of data.

These examples of the experiences of mediums relating to and communicating with others has at least demonstrated that surely here is a rich field for telepathic research. Too often are mediums belittled or accused of trickery; there has never yet been any sustained, large-scale data collection in the various areas, such as clairaudience or individual sittings with clients; neither have mediums been interviewed sympathetically and at length.

Mesmerism and hypnotism

Before plunging into the adventures and findings of those who practised hypnosis and discerned links with telepathy, it might be cautionary to begin with critical opinion: for there are those who are lifelong students of the mysterious technique who do not even acknowledge that telepathy exists.

Such a critic is H.H. Gibson, one of the leading British experts on the subject, who is a well-qualified academic and engaged on work with the Nuffield Hypnosis Research Unit. In his book, *Hypnosis*, written in 1977, he maintains that alleged connections between hypnosis and telepathy were initially suggested by such novelists as Poe, George du Maurier, Melville and Dickens. He makes the following relevant points:

> Many readers may be surprised to learn that the evidence for the very existence of telepathy is by no means good . . . .

> Because so many people are wedded to their personal telepathy story it is difficult for them to be open-minded about the subject to admit to themselves that perhaps chance and coincidence played a role in what was happening and to ask (a sensitive question) has the story perhaps grown in the telling of it . . .?

> In the opinion of Professor C.E.M. Hansel there is not a shred of scientifically acceptable evidence to support belief in telepathy.

It is with these caveats in mind that the data given in the bulk of this chapter, as elsewhere, might be considered. Gibson may be cautious in posing a null hypothesis, but at least this means that believers will have to present sound evidence; too often, material offered in parapsychological matters is anecdotal and thus personal, with all the disadvantages mentioned above. (One is reminded of the French system of justice in which an accused is judged guilty until proved innocent.) It is to be hoped, however, that critics such as Gibson will not be unduly blinkered by their own prejudices and that if positive patterns emerge from cases independent^ly reported over, say, a century or so, then they may reconsider their viewpoints.

In early Victorian England mesmerism (dubbed hypnotism or nervous sleep by Braid) was totally discounted by the leading medical journal, *The Lancet*: 'Mesmerism is too gross a humbug to admit of any further serious notice. We regard its abetters as quacks and impostors. They ought to be hooted out of professional society' (29 October 1842).

A first consideration might be the life of Franz Anton Mesmer (1734-1815), in order to examine the origins of the practice to which he gave his name and which roused such a choleric reaction from his peers a quarter of a century or so after his death; for Mesmer was, from first to last, a doctor and healer and his theories on hypnotic phenomena were secondary to his chosen activities. He was born on 23 May 1734, on the German border near Lake Constance, with the Swiss Alps away on the southern skyline. His father was a gamekeeper and a devout Catholic, the family being respectable and rather above the peasant class. He spent much of his boyhood in, as the saying goes, solitary contemplation of nature, with magnificent opportunities for so doing. Whether or not, as he suggested, this resulted in a certain elevation of spirit, as in the case of Wordsworth and the English Lakes, can never be established, but his ideas of some universal spiritual essence in humans, capable of uniting mankind akin to Sir Oliver Lodge's concept of ether (see page 169), may have been sensed on his early wanderings. In his *Propositions Asserted*, published in his heyday in Vienna in the 1780s, he describes it thus:

1. There exists a mutual influence between the heavenly bodies, the earth and animate bodies.

2. A universally distributed fluid, so continuous as to admit of

no vacuums anywhere . . . this is the medium of the influence.

The animal, or human, body thus sustained itself by taking this fluid 'into the substance of the nerves' and variable capacities to store up, concentrate or transmit the magnetic fluid resulted in some individuals being more able than others to heal maladies. 'This property of the animal body,' he wrote in Proposition 10, 'which brings it under the influence of heavenly bodies and the reciprocal action of those surrounding it, as shown by the analogy with the Magnet, induced me to term it Animal Magnetism'. Humans could thus be magnetically interconnected and perhaps cured of ills; practitioners themselves, especially of strongly magnetic potential, could influence and cure others. Naively, he imagined that the future professionals, far from hooting at him as was *The Lancet* later to do, would judge him favourably:

> Physicians, being the repositories of public trust for everything connected with the preservation and happiness of mankind, are alone enabled by the knowledge on which their profession is founded, to judge of the importance of the discovery I have just announced and realise its implications. In a word, they alone are qualified to put it into practice.

Alas, his optimism was ill-founded. Even in his lifetime successive enquiries into his systems of curing the sick, his establishments and rituals of carrying out his treatment and, not least, his flamboyant personality (he would have been a godsend to any television company today) – these, often headed by eminent medical men of the time, pronounced his theories misguided and his practises undesirable. Close body contact, stroking, the induction of hysterical states before curing by hypnotism, and public acclaim in which he enjoyed basking all led to his undoing.

In his fashionable salon in Paris between 1778 and 1785 he was visited by people from all walks of life, from the very poor to the aristocracy – all of whom received parity of attention. However, he inclined towards a certain commercial realism, as the description of his salon by his biographer Buranelli (1976) suggests:

There were four baquets in the large room, three for those who could pay and one for the indigent. As the patients arrived they were examined, given whatever preliminary treatment Mesmer considered necessary, and escorted by his assistants to their places around one or other of the baquets. They took hold of the protruding bars leading up from the magnetized water, touched the ends with their ailing bodies, or held hands to set up a 'current' of animal magnetism, and waited for the healing process to begin.

Mesmer presided. He maintained the proper presence for the occasion, the 'bedside manner' of the Mesmerian seance, appearing in a powdered wig with a coat and breeches of purple silk, ruffles of lace at his wrists, shining buckled shoes on his feet. In his right hand he carried a wand, usually of wrought iron. Moving through the room from baquet to baquet, from patient to patient, he kept an eye on how each was progressing.

Such reports as that of a commission held in 1784 led to his eventual departure from the capital. The unanimous judgement by his peers was that he propounded ideas of 'a non-existent fluid without utility', of 'imagination provoked into action' (or auto-suggestion) and a summarising statement that 'all group treatment where the methods of magnetism are employed must have, in the long run, harmful effects'.

So Mesmer moved on from Paris in 1785 and spent the next few years wandering around Europe and demonstrating his curative powers; there is no doubt that his healing successes were generally recognised, but his theoretical base of the universal magnetic fluid met with much scepticism. At fifty-nine he went back to Lake Constance to settle down at last, and spent the last years of his life around his boyhood haunts, being often visited by neo-mesmerists who sought the opinions of the master. His influence was considerable, and Buranelli has dubbed him 'the Columbus of psychology', maintaining that 'his impress is clear on psychiatry, psychosomatic medicine, personality studies and group therapy'. Yet within the context of the little explored area of telepathy and hypnotism his influence was even more profound shortly after his death than it was later in the more conventional areas of academic psychology. Le Cron (1970) noted that at points in his writings Mesmer often commented

upon sympathetic sensations and thought-links between mes-
merisers and patients, and even stated that somnambulists could
distinctly see the past, present and future. Furthermore,
Mesmer maintained that on occasion his entranced patients
could not only read his thoughts as they came to his mind but
could also tell him what he was about to say.

It is next of relevance to deal with the career of a doctor
named John Elliotson, who was an ardent mesmerist and
performed painless operations at University College Hospital
London, which he had helped to found in 1834. By 1838
missionary activities were conducted with such zeal by this
vigorous and somewhat eccentric character that the Hospital
Committee resolved 'to take such steps as they shall deem most
advisable, to prevent the practice of Mesmerism or Animal
Magnetism in the future within the Hospital'. One step was, of
course, to invite Elliotson to resign, which he did.

He founded, and edited successfully for twenty years, a
magazine called *The Zoist*, which favoured equally the doctrines
of the mystic Swedenborg and Mesmer. It was subtitled 'A
Journal of Cerebral Physiology and Mesmerism and their
application to Human Welfare' and had a salient quotation
from Dr. Gall, the venerable physician, on its frontispiece: 'This
is *Truth*, though opposed to the Philosophy of the Age'.

There are in the journal many reports of the successes of
doctors using mesmeric methods and purifying or replenishing
the animal magnetism latent in humans. There are also several
interesting accounts of the extraordinary rapport subsisting
between doctor and patient, and specific instances not only of
empathy of sensation but also the ability of the percipient to
discern thoughts in the mind of the agent or mesmeriser. One
such is written by a Dr. G. Bush of New York in 1847. He
describes how after he had entranced one lady somebody nearby
inadvertently stood on his foot. He winced with the sudden pain
– as did the mesmerised patient. He then experimented by
eating cheese, asked the patient what taste she experienced, and
was told cheese. He also held a ticking watch to his ear, and on
checking what his patient could hear, found that she experienced the same sensation. He writes:

On still another occasion I requested her to describe what I was then contemplating in my own mind – a torch-light procession on Broadway. She spoke of the banners, the mottoes of which she tried to read, the horses, the multitudes of people, saying 'there's no end to them'. In all these cases she had no clue whatever to my thoughts except the thoughts themselves . . . .

Bush throws a novel light on the subject of Mesmerism when he writes on the subject of thought-bonds between the doctor and entranced patient:

I have tried scores of similar experiments with similar successes. The fact which we have above considered – the transfer of thought – may be regarded as the cardinal fact of the Mesmeric developments. In the whole category of its marvels there is nothing more wonderful – nothing more difficult to believe, yet nothing more easy to prove.

Perhaps some of the most decisive experiments carried out, were those involving mesmerised patients, reacting to phrenological promptings. Phrenology, that alleged science which links surface areas of the skull with the development and position of organs of mental faculties (such as veneration, combativeness, benevolence and so forth), was much in vogue at the time. Even today it is possible to find practitioners of this ancient study, who often display model heads with the various areas marked out. 'Having your bumps read' was still a feature of character delineation at the turn of the nineteenth century, although belief (and any validating studies) are both hard to find at the present time.

One of the common procedures with mesmerised patients was to touch particular areas on a marked phrenological cranium and observe the reaction in the percipient. Here is a rather amusing account of one such episode involving Bush and other parties; the telepathic undertones are obvious:

I mesmerised Serena Price, through a wall at a distance of twenty yards. She fell asleep in two minutes and produced beautiful and striking manifestations of the whole of the phrenological organs marked on a bust . . . a gentleman not satisfied about phreno mesmerism, spied his opportunity when my back was turned, to excite combativeness when she immediately sprang from her chair and knocked down a medical gentleman that was feeling her pulse at the time. This simple circumstance converted both himself and the doctor.

At the time, of course, several doctors were concentrating upon this or that phrenological area of the skull, and the patient duly obliged.

Confirmation of the results of the above type of experiment comes from records in the 1840s of none other than Dr. James Braid, who actually coined the word 'hypnotism', suggesting that the greatest attention should always be upon the suggestibility of the patient and on the nervous sleep (or deeper nervous coma, in which it was possible to carry out surgical operations) rather than to explain such phenomena by travelling down the blind alleys of animal magnetism, in which he, like the Parisian investigators of Mesmer, could not believe. He carried out several experiments in the area of 'phreno-hypnotic' phenomena, under the profound impression that he was validating phrenology rather than indicating that there might be thought-links between a doctor and his patient in a hypnotic condition.

Now Braid was a Scot and a deeply religious man, after the manner of many mid-Victorians of the professional classes. He believed in the importance of the soul as well as the body, and saw the mind (somewhat unconventionally by modern medical standards, as being distinct from the brain, the relationship being that of a 'commanding officer to his troops'. The hypnotic trance, or rather the hypnotic coma as he later came to see the profounder levels of hypnotism, was an example of the mind achieving dominance over the body and manipulating the nervous system. There were thus somewhat religious undertones, if not overtones, to his zealous pursuit of curing by hypnotic methods.

Braid was also a firm believer in phrenology, as were Bush and Elliotson who recorded their findings in *The Zoist*, and he experimented with patients under hypnosis in order to verify his ideas. Here is an account of one such experiment, taken from the A.E. Waite edition of 1899 of the writings of Braid:

I placed a cork endways over the organ of veneration, and

bound it in that position by a bandage passing under the chin. I now hypnotized the patient, and observed the effect, which was precisely the same, for some time, as when no such appliance was used; after a minute and a half had elapsed, an altered expression of countenance took place, and a move- ment of the arms and hands, which latter became clasped in adoration, and the patient now arose from the seat and knelt down as if engaged in prayer. On moving the cork forwards, active benevolence was manifested, and on being pushed back, veneration again manifested itself. I have repeatedly tried similar experiments with this, and other patients, with the like results, including other organs.

The patients, usually, had no phrenological knowledge, yet Braid knew the areas of the skull associated with behaviours and, as described above, might well have entertained expect- ations about his patients' reactions. Thus ideas from the mind of the diligent doctor may have been received by the patient: the only alternative to this hypothesis is that phrenology has been proven by these experiments, which has not been accepted in the twentieth century. Thus the experiences of Braid, and others, concerning the notion that hypnotism and telepathy may be powerfully linked may not be so remote as conventional critics would have us believe.

The main exponent of animal magnetism, following Mesmer, was Baron von Reichenbach (1788–1869). He was a dis- tinguished German industrial chemist, the inventor of creosote, and also a rich nobleman. After making a fortune in business, he retired to his castle to conduct lengthy and rigorous experiments involving sensitives and their perceptions of what he believed to be vital emanations from humans – the 'odylic force', to use his terminology. This force was akin to the lines of magnetism radiating from magnets, an aura of vitality that could be amplified by magnetic treatment or used as a medium for thought-transference, as described by Dr. William Gregory in his book *Animal Magnetism* published in Edinburgh in 1851.

In it homage is duly paid to Reichenbach as a painstaking investigator, and the Scots doctor outlines the advantages of study in relation to disease thus:

Animal magnetism operates chiefly on the nervous system

and is therefore applicable chiefly or most naturally, to nervous diseases, such as Hysteria, Catalepsy, Convulsions, paralysing both the nerves of motion and those of sensation, Neuralgia, Insanity &c &c.

Although this kind of statement seems a throwback to the cures of Mesmer seventy years before, there are links with Braid, the hard-headed opponent of Reichenbach, who maintained that, far from discovering some new magnetic force, the German had mistaken the subject's influence on his own nervous system for some mythical outside force. This represents a very interesting theoretical development, and Braid stated his case thus:

It is an undoubted fact that with many individuals, and especially of the highly nervous and imaginative and ab-stractive classes, a strong direction of inward consciousness to any part of the body, especially if attended with the expectation or belief of something being about to happen, is quite sufficient to change the physical action of the part, and to produce such an impression from this cause alone, as Baron Reichenbach attributes to his new force.

So Braid truly outlined the enormous force of auto-suggestion and its effect on the nervous system. This is well-illustrated from many accounts of the superhuman strength of people under stress, in the nervously disturbed, or violently insane.

But Gregory maintains that magnetic forces *may* flow from a mesmeriser to a patient and, besides affecting cures, may also serve as media for the transfer of thoughts. Ideas, in fact, flow from one nerve aura to another. There is thus a demonstrable input of cerebral activity from the agent into the mind of the receiver. By some sympathetic rapport created betweeen nerve auras, then, a channel is formed along which information might flow, facilitated by radiations of odylic force from sender and receiver; and, although Gregory's theoretical position may be classified as an invisible wave theory, he gives a rather striking and unusual case as evidence for the existence of odylic force transmitted not only from doctor to patient but vice-versa. Gregory states that a Dr. Atkinson was treating a lady, by mesmerism, for a nervous tic and she had to go to Paris and cease treatment. He hit on the idea of sending her a mesmerised glove by post.

> The experiment succeeded perfectly, the glove put on her hand always sent her into mesmeric sleep, and relieved her intense suffering, which all other means had wholly failed to do. The mesmerised glove by use gradually lost its property, and then failed to cause sleep, after a third time; so that I had to send newly mesmerised gloves every week, and the old ones were from time to time returned, to be charged afresh. This led to the observation of a very striking fact . . . I felt in my hand, on approaching the old gloves, the same unpleasant sensations I have from touching a diseased individual, besides absolute pain from the tic . . . .

Atkinson checked also that relief was not due to auto-suggestion by sending both unmesmerised gloves and used gloves: on receipt of the former no healing effect was felt, and receipt of the latter had 'a most disagreeable effect'. He also carried out other well-nigh unbelievable experiments involving gloves: 'On one occasion I breathed a dream into a glove which I sent to a lady – the dream occurred'.

Here, indeed, are we into neglected parapsychological pastures. Gregory and Atkinson agree with Elliotson and Bush of *The Zoist*: cures affected by personal magnetism, animal magnetism – or by the effect of the elusive odylic force of Reichenbach – were not due, as critics of Mesmer's baquets supposed, to over-roused imaginations, but to the tangible action of some outside semi-physical force upon nervous systems.

Is there any day-to-day evidence of such an effect?

It is possible that minor versions of the process occur at all times and places whenever people meet interaction. The medium Rosalind Heywood, in her book *The Infinite Hive*, wrote:

> Even when they do not know it men and women are reacting all the time to elements in their immediate vicinity which are not perceptible to their five senses . . . beneath the surface we are in constant telepathic communication with each other,

proportionately to the mental or emotional affinity between particular individuals.

We all know the difference between being with somebody with whom we are in tune and can relax, and having to apply ourselves to socially related behaviour where we win or lose variously in commercial or personal situations; much often depends on whether we feel uncertain or in a position to dominate; and the unspoken wishes or feelings come through the words exchanged or the situation. Consider the effect that the presence and will of Napoleon had on the hulking French General Vandamme, described by Le Bon as a 'rough, typical soldier of the Revolution';

> That devil of a man exercises a fascination on me that I cannot explain even to myself, and in such a degree that, though I fear neither God or devil, when I am in his presence I am ready to tremble like a child; and he could make me go through the eye of a needle to throw myself in the fire. . . .

Hypnotism, supposed magnetic fluids radiated by humans, presences, forces and auras go back a long way. What is of relevance to this chapter is not only an examination of cases involving transmissions and receptions of unspoken words, states and ideas, but also any explanations which have been offered down the years as to *how* or *why* this should happen. In other words, to ascend or descend to jargon depending on your viewpoint, our examination must include both speculation and evidence from the five senses.

Almost at the end of the nineteenth century, in 1892, A.P. Sinnett came back strongly against the critics of Mesmer and *Animal Magnetism* in his book entitled *The Rationale of Mesmerism*. He was a founder member of the Theosophical Society, a scholar, and had aristocratic connections, like many interested in the development of parapsychology at that time. He was especially interested in the more mystical aspects of Theosophy, as some of his book titles (*Esoteric Buddhism, Karma, The Occult World*) indicate. He wrote, most positively, in favour of the existence of a 'magnetic fluid' which could pass between individuals, and made no bones as to who were the villains of the piece:

Many mesmerists of the higher order entertain no doubt concerning the existence of this fluid, for the simple reason that they can see it . . . a well known writer, Baron von Reichenbach, devoted himself especially to this branch of mesmeric inquiry. He has recorded with patient care, for which a pig-headed generation inhabiting the earth about the middle of this century gave him no gratitude, a long series of results obtained with a great many 'sensitives' whom he employed, all having to do with their power of seeing visible emanations from human fingers, as also from physical magnetic apparatus.

Sinnett was thus in direct opposition to Braid as to the perceptions of sensitives: just as Mesmer's critics claimed that auto-suggestion was a prime factor in the curative powers of the rods and baquets, so did Reichenbach's investigators (and there were many) ascribe observations of human effluvia to the same human source: we see what we want to see and man is the measure of all things.

But at least Sinnett suggested a model for the transmission of ideas from agent to percipient, notably in the case of inducing magnetic or hypnotic sleep. Indeed, he suggested that this magnetic model was in fact reality:

If he is endeavouring to induce a trance, the mesmerist must keep that idea in view, not bothering himself for the moment as to what may follow after, but simply imagining in his own mind that from his hand a rain of subtle soporific influence is descending and drenching the nervous organism of the sensitive. Perhaps it may enable anyone who tries, to realise this idea in his imagination all the better, if the study of these pages may have induced him to comprehend and believe, what is an actual fact, that such an influence does descend under the conditions imposed.

Sinnett makes use of his concept of the aura, or psychic surround mentioned above, when he puts forward a process whereby sensory impressions may be conveyed from the mesmeriser to the subject. He mentions that there are many examples of such transmissions, giving as an instance an operator silently reading a book at one end of a room while the mesmerised subject reads the words as they pass across the field of vision of the other. He sums up the whole process thus:

> The establishment of the mesmeric condition has set up magnetic relations between the auras of the two persons concerned, and the conditions of consciousness acquired by the operator through his own senses, and then by a natural automatic process reflected in his own aura, are equally reflected in the aura of the subject, and thence directly transferred to those innermost centres of consciousness which the subject's senses are able to approach, and which, therefore, when excited in his own nature, seem to him to have been excited in the ordinary way.

An important point is that the emphasis in the telepathic process thus shifts to the percipient playing the more active role or, as Mrs. Sidgwick concluded after studying telepathy experiments '. . . . the role of the so-called agent is merely passive, and it is the percipient who plays the active role in extracting an idea or combination of ideas from the mind of the agent'.

There is a case for using the phrase, preferred by some French investigators, *metagnomy*; this means, literally, knowledge shared, knowledge outside the five senses, and implies that this is as much a quest on the part of the perceiver as impulses directed by the sender. The word 'telepathy', as the chemist, Sir Charles Richet has pointed out, suggests messages being sent from a distance, rather than a coincidence of mind states.

In the mesmeric, or hypnotic trance, then, conditions for such rapports are facilitated. In the theatre, of course, a mass audience also makes for greater heightening of emotional tension as will be outlined in the next chapter, where experiences of both genuine and fraudulent stage telepathists are examined.

[5]
Stage telepathy

In the first chapter of this book a brief and introductory visit was paid to the intriguing area of public wonder and its titillation by various illusionists; the point was made that scientific outlooks on telepathy tend to associate the subject with such long standing trickery. We might now, however, consider the whole area of stage telepathy more closely, not only to speculate as to how effects are produced, but also to examine a less commonly researched feature – that there may be a genuine telepathic phenomenon involved in such performances.

Any public gathering involving a performer, or orator, and an audience, carries with it an aura of the mystical, for rapport between the speaker and each individual before him is all important. Obviously, the time, place and social context contribute to the success of the occasion, but over and above these is the personality of the individual upon whom the audience's attention is concentrated, and his power to sway the emotions or move the opinions of those before him. Such authority was termed 'charismatic' by the German sociologist Max Weber at the beginning of the century, and the word 'charisma' has passed, to be used copiously, into our everyday vocabulary. In the case of the stage magician presenting a thought-reading act, this personal aura of mystery and magnetism is essential.

One of the most notorious and colourful of stage telepathists was the charismatic Walford Bodie (1869 to 1939) who was assisted in his act over many years by his wife and sister. He was internationally famous and Houdini spoke of 'taking a Bodie' (trying a long shot) in his telepathy act with Bess in the late 1890s when the Scots magician was still a comparatively young man and at the height of his fame. Chaplin, in his early

Walford Bodie (1862–1939), stage telepathist and healer

autobiography, included a photograph of himself made up to look like Bodie, complete with waxed moustache and hypnotic stare; the year would be about 1905. It seems, at first sight, that Bodie performed well in carnival tradition and was a conjuror after all, albeit a highly successful one. But was he merely that? Was there more to Bodie than unusually impudent chicanery? Perhaps.

Consider first this extract taken from one of his books, entitled *The Bodie Book* and published in 1905:

Walford Bodie, as caricatured by a young Charles Chaplin who referred to him as 'a well-known quack'

On the stage! Face to face with the public! Ah! that means a lot to me. The stage is the gateway to my world – the world where I come in touch with the great British people to show them what I can do and how to do it. It is my arena, where I face all difficulties and issue challenges to my enemies. The lights, the music, the sea of eager faces – these are like champagne to me. The scene and its surroundings stimulate those forces in me which I combine with electricity to perform

my cures. And that is why my success is always greatest on the
stage.

His obvious enthusiasm shines out beacon-like from such a
passage and, indeed, this zeal for performing sustained him in
the music-halls for over forty years – a long time indeed for a
stage performer. He also demonstrated healing, the spectacular
generation and transmission of electric charges on-stage (a
novelty in the Nineties certainly), and was a formidable
hypnotist.

His book is written from the viewpoint of a vigorous
missionary, agog to establish the reality of such borderline areas
as clairvoyance, telepathy, mental suggestion and 'magnetic
touch'. The photograph on page 90, in best Edwardian 'before
and after' fashion, will be a source of risibility for critics and give
food for thought to others. Certainly he was eager to heal, and
the following passage seems to carry a certain vocational
fervour:

> Now the curtain is rung down. But my work is not yet over.
> There is still much to do. And this is where I take off my coat
> and tackle as many of the cases waiting at the stage door as I
> can get through before the stage manager insists on closing
> the theatre. I take them as they come, and – well, it is hard
> work, but my heart is in it.
>
> When closing time arrives I tell those that are still waiting
> to come on the morrow at two o'clock when I will attend to
> them. Finally I pass out at the stage door where there is still a
> crowd all clamouring to greet me, and as I drive away I hear
> their blessings shouted after me – the blessings of those whose
> friends or relations I have cured.

Yet the opinions of other artists, such as Chaplin (who was
touring music-halls at the time with a Fred Karno troupe of
comics), cannot be ignored. Bodie may well have had the streak
of a saint in him, but it is likely he had recourse to signalling and
prepared set pieces which he does not dwell on in his vigorous
book. At the back of *The Bodie Book* are to be found advertise-
ments, typical of 1905, which hint, to put it charitably, at a
certain medicinal over-enthusiasm:

The Bodie Electric Drug Co.
Sole Patentees of ELECTRIC RUB,
an oleaginous liniment compound
of various alkaloids and organic
salts the action of which upon the
skin is electrical.
The Greatest Discovery of the Age.
ELECTRIC LIFE PILLS.
Renews youth and vigour.

Mystic Marie, as his sister was called on the playbills, would sketch as willed by Bodie while hypnotized and blindfolded; she would also sit blindfolded with her back to a blackboard on which were written numbers and names. Under the silent watch of her wax-moustached brother, who stood above her with outstretched hands executing magnetic passes, she would call out figures and words as he pointed to the board. She would play, blindfolded, tunes at the piano transmitted by her brother, who would then pass down in the audience, stopping or starting the recital with a wave of his hand. Enthusiasts would claim that other hypnotic cases show a similar control by the agent over percipient, but many would draw attention to the wide possibilities of visual signalling from others acting as anonymous intermediaries; there is also the ever-present matter of the quality of the blindfold.

Even so, there are still those who remember Bodie from his famous days, and attest to his powers as a hypnotist; could he not have mesmerised his sister (psychic links between siblings are common enough) and willed her to stop playing the piano? Experiments of such a nature are common enough according to reports from both Russian and European research in this century.

It is likely, then, that there will always be this division of opinion about the credibility of professed stage telepathists. It is not only audience members who ascribe psychic powers to performers, but also men of the calibre of Conan Doyle and Oliver Lodge. Both these altruistic and industrious researchers came in for considerable criticism from cynics, who cited them as examples of how academics could easily be fooled by carny men and other illusionists; Houdini went as far as to say that those

The power of suggestion
(*left*) 'Before treatment the patient cannot lift half an ounce'
(*right*) Bodie in action

from the 'ivory towers' could be fooled more easily than the public who, after all, had to make their living in the hard day-to-day world.

One of the more interesting interactions in this connection is the encounter between Sir Oliver Lodge and the Zancigs. These performers had a verbal code which was used so often that, towards the end of their days, members of the audience would call out the key to some words relating to objects supposedly transmitted to the blindfolded Mrs. Zancig. In 1907, however, they were held in good repute, and Lodge describes sitting in the balcony when Zancig came along, seeking words for transmission to his wife down on the stage. The scientist recorded the incident thus:

> I handed him a piece of paper on which I had written the word 'Istapalapan'. I took care he should not see the word previously to my giving him the paper. Zancig remarked to me in a whisper, 'This is a long word'. Owing to the distance from his wife it could not have been possible for her to overhear these words. Then Mr. Zancig called out, 'Spell this'. Madam Zancig immediately wrote on the blackboard which was on the stage, 'Istpala'.

Critics would immediately point to Zancig heightening the performance atmosphere by using hesitation, the possibility of visual signalling, either directly to his wife or to an accomplice who might act as an intermediary. Lodge, however, inferred that telepathy might have taken place.

Tests carried out in private, where the Zancigs operated under test conditions separated by a screen, resulted in the reproduction of drawings transmitted from man to wife; Zancig also admitted to Lodge that the two made use of codes but that, from time to time, there existed a flashing sympathy between them which was 'more efficient and quicker than anything they could get by codes'. This certainly accords with many experiences between couples, siblings and other family members, but such data are generally unrecorded on any scale; it may be argued, of course, that coincidence, mis-reporting and wanting to believe in the wondrous and mystical loom large, but kinship telepathic links (especially among non-industrialized peoples) appear to manifest from time to time.

Any consideration of stage telepathy would be incomplete without a mention of one of the most famous acts of recent times – that of the Piddingtons, whose radio performances in 1949 attracted huge listening audiences; television had not yet come into general use, and the appeal of wireless to the imagination was strong. Here is an account from Russell Braddon's book *The Piddingtons* (1950) describing a highlight of one of the programmes; in this particular setting Lesley is in the Bloody Tower at the Tower of London and her husband is in a BBC studio where actor Dennis Price has just written 'Be abandoned as the electricians said that they would leave no current' on a blackboard for Sydney to transmit:

> 'Men . . . light . . .' and the test which was to make the Piddingtons the greatest source of argument in the whole of Britain was on its way . . . 'Electricians,' she announced in the voice of one who knows it's silly but that's what she thinks. All over Britain people sat a little closer to the edge of their chairs and decided that things were getting interesting. Would she get the rest? What would happen next?
>
> Their answer was twenty seconds of complete silence which all the radio experts in England had previously announced quite authoritatively could never hold any audience. This night it held twenty million.

And, of course, in the end:

> Word followed word, vague impressions became articulate, and finally, with some ninety seconds to spare before the allotted time on the air had run itself out, Lesley spoke the complete line . . . back in the studio, the audience, technicians, Freddie Piffard, the producer of the show, and Colin Wills, its most excellent commentator, applauded as only those who are both acutely pleased and acutely relieved can applaud.

Yet there are still those today, thirty years after, who wonder whether the Piddingtons were 'genuine'. A simple answer is that the BBC does not risk money, time and its reputation on

The Piddingtons
This carefully posed publicity photograph emphasizes the need in
1949 for glamour and mystery in telepathy acts

programmes where outcomes are uncertain. Even the most sensitive of percipients cannot guarantee a 100-per-cent accuracy, and on that score alone it is highly probable that the Piddingtons, their manager Russell Braddon, and especially the producer of the show, used some form of code, set piece, or accomplices, these three being the most common devices from past stage telepathy performers. When all three are combined together, detection is well nigh impossible.

Lesley was a highly skilled actress (note the twenty second pause and the timing, finishing ninety seconds before the time limit) and all involved in the radio performance appreciated the need for a lively presentation, in terms of settings and suspense. To quote again from Braddon's book and Sydney Piddington:

> If those broadcasts start cold they won't go at all! We've got to get people telepathy conscious before they start; and we must have people fighting about it after they start, so that the controversy's kept boiling. If there's no controversy, we're a flop!

Yet the whole idea of the act had started some sixteen years before in a Japanese prison, where Braddon and Piddington were cruelly used as slave labour. By chance, they had come across a magazine article on J.B. Rhine and his activities at Duke University in the States, and began trying tests to pass away the Malayan evening in Changi Jail. Two sentences from Braddon are unusually explicit and suggest that he and Piddington could certainly score significantly in such experiments:

> We passed from the stage of poor results and frivolity to good results and an absorbed interest. Consistently, and without speaking, moving or looking, either one at the other, we passed correctly colours and numbers and numbers and objects indicated by a third person.

It will be noted that there is no mention of thought-transference here. It could be that the two perfected an ingenious code – or even that a third person was involved. On the other hand, believers in telepathic development might argue that practice improved performance.

Braddon, now a spry sixty-year-old and a best-selling international author, never wrote again on the subject of telepathy
after his book on the Piddingtons, most of his works being
biographical and political. Had he been a genuine telepathist,
surely he would have written more of the Changi experiments
and more details of the adventures of Sydney and Lesley. He
described Piddington as 'forceful, confident, knew what he
wanted to do, knew how he thought he could do it, knew exactly
the measure of his ability.' Lesley, the daughter of a rear-
admiral, was 'at the top of her profession as a radio actress before
she was twenty-one'. So the famous pair were invited to perform
for a week at the London Palladium on the strength of eight
successful BBC shows, and toured the provinces. A further three
radio shows followed, and they returned to their native
Australia. Television arrived, the music-hall declined further,
and it may be that they were, in fact, the last of the old-fashioned
husband-and-wife telepathy stage acts.

An intriguing American performer is Kreskin. He was born in
New Jersey in 1930; and (in Bodie tradition) is a stage hypnotist
and a telepathist. He graduated in psychology and, besides stage
performances, works in business and in the community. He does
not claim to be a psychic but in an interview published in the
American magazine *Psychic* he disclosed that his performances,
in which he reads off information selected by audiences, or has
them onstage choosing pages and items from a book or stopping
watches at specified times, are a blend of conjuring, suggestibility and ESP. He denies using any confederates whatsoever.
He estimates the conjuring element at ten to fifteen per cent,
suggestibility at fifty per cent, and the balance to ESP.

'If I'm having difficulty establishing rapport with my audience,' he commented, 'the ESP portion could be only twenty per
cent, but it can climb to sixty-five per cent when the audience
and I are in tune – I can roll on and on. Also, I discovered I had
to condition my audience, which is really the secret of what I do'.
He describes his ESP experience thus:

> Images appear to me commonly with my eyes open, as I'm
> looking over an audience. In the case of reading a social
> security number, I see it in a sequence more easily over a
> darkened part of the theatre, which acts like a black board for

me. I don't see with my mind, but I can project the number with my eyes open, visualize the numbers instantly . . . if I start to evaluate critically, I destroy whatever I'm getting naturally. It has come impulsively, spontaneously, which is in itself the kind of training you have to learn to harness.

Other points made by the international performer are as under:

> Science shouldn't have to stay in the laboratory, because the emotional factor, a key ingredient in the whole field, is so often left out of the laboratory and you cannot easily create emotions there. . . .

> Dr. Rhine and his work were twenty years ahead of his time and made a great contribution. Today, however, I think they are twenty years behind the time. . . .

> Sure, I take a one-mile walk before every television show or concert to detach myself from the distractions of things around me and to build up an attitude of deep introspection . . . perhaps in terms of your readers what I do is 'psych' myself up.

Yet if he is asked whether he is a psychic he will deny this. He maintains that the ingredients he uses in his concerts are conjuring, thought-perception, telepathic phenomena, sub-conscious sensitivity, suggestibility and humour.'

He is, if you like, a modern stage telepathist.

6

In crowds

In the history of mankind crowd behaviour has often played important roles in the establishing or sustaining of regimes, whether it be the French in 1789, the Germans at Nazi rallies in the 1930s, or the British crowd outside Buckingham Palace on VE day a decade later. Extremes of emotional states spread swiftly, take hold, and demand some physical means of discharge – in our own times the truculence of young football supporters is a socially disruptive manifestation.

Little progress by way of explaining theoretically crowd behaviour, or of tracing the generation and mechanisms of transmission of heightened feelings, has emerged down the years. Such classic books on human behaviour as *The Crowd* by Le Bon or *The Instincts of the Herd in War and Peace* by Trotter have acquainted us with plenty of examples of mobs, both euphoric and savage, but it is not easy to move on to why and how such conditions originate, develop and disappear. For one thing, terminology is hard to come by: what is the definition of a crowd, in what numbers do the participants form, how might these elusive currents be traced? Such questions seemingly defeat the best of scientific investigations.

At the risk of being tiresomely pedantic, if not etymologically nitpicking, might I suggest that the word telepathy, well though it has served us this hundred years, be extended for the purpose of this chapter? In crowds and mobs, transmitted meanings are mostly of an emotional nature, so might I suggest the word 'telempathy' for the transmission of feelings between humans, as opposed to words and ideas, these being largely associated with 'telepathy'? The subtle spread of these mass movements (emotional states are often accompanied by fluid movements in the physical body) is often so intense and distinctive that I would think a separate word altogether might be coined, in order to so describe a form of telepathy, which itself suggests both words and bodily states.

It seems at first glance that emotions are roused by visual, aural and rhythmic stimuli acting upon an individual nervous system. The British see a Union Jack and experience pride or otherwise, as others do at the sight of the Hammer and Sickle or the Swastika. Not for nothing was the standard-bearer, or flag-carrier, a key member of any army.

The immediate, possibly extra-sensory, effect which in-dividual behaviour can have on a crowd (and vice-versa) is perhaps most poignantly illustrated in the case of a performer and his audience. Within a very short while any entertainer, particularly, must assess the mood of his scrutinizers, and no more so than in the case of a comedian. In my pursuit of possible effects of audiences on performers, I once asked the comic Terry Scott whether he was able to assess audience atmosphere when coming on to the stage. The talk ran roughly thus:

'After about ten minutes in, say, a farce, surely it is possible to tell whether the audience is receptive or not . . . the laughter alone should tell you?'

'Ten seconds is enough. It's something you feel when you walk on. You don't need laughter, or lack of it, to tell whether an audience is on your side. Somehow you know when you walk on.'

'Perhaps you are unconsciously rationalizing a seen or heard response. It must vary from one individual to another, percep-tion of atmosphere?'

'Not much. You can tell. We used to have a code. If it was going to be all right you'd come walking off after a first exit and tip off the actor coming on with a number from one to a hundred. Eighty for very good and twenty for bloody awful, hard going.' I got the idea.

'Well, Scott went on, 'one night I played a joke on a fella. The audience was dead cold and I gave him a 75 and on he went, all breezy, expecting a great reception and down he went. 75 indeed.'

Receptive atmospheres in audiences soon become persuasive and such is contagion of merriment, that only the slightest of cues is needed by the performer to bring out even more raucous gales of laughter. This description of what, by present-day standards, must surely be but modestly funny humour illustrates the point. It is taken from an 1874 volume entitled *The Wilds of London* and its author, James Greenwood, was clearly not attracted by the early music-hall or its performers; he described Ezekiah Podgers, a famous comic, singing his song thus:

> It came to this as the fifth verse declared:
> She shoved me right bang into a dish of
> fried Dutch plaice.
> Took hold of a bowl of butter, and threw
> it in my face;
> The driver came in at the time, to make
> my troubles complete,
> He got all the boys to pelt me as I ran
> away down the street.
> Doodle de dum, doodle de doodle lum, de
> doodle lum, de doodle lay.

The last line is the refrain of this exquisitely humorous ditty but the people couldn't sing it for laughing. They tried, but the recollection of the catastrophe just related was too much for them, and they broke down to roar and bang the table and ring the glasses with the liquor stirrers, and cry 'Encore' as though but a little more of Ezekiah Podgers were required to fill their chalice of earthly bliss and restore them to old Eden.

Nearer our own times there was Harry Lauder, dressed as a schoolmaster, before a board with chalk in hand. 'A wee bit o' chalk', he would say gravely to his audience, and the Glasgow folk would be almost bent double with hysterical laughter. (The same type of audience was to howl down Mark Sheridan, for whom the song 'I do like to be beside the seaside' was written in 1917. After the performance the melancholy comedian went walking in a nearby park and committed suicide by shooting himself. Such, again, is the power of King Mob over the performer, and the generator of humour must, by the nature of his job, be one of the more sensitive of humans.) All of us could recall comics holding audiences and eliciting gales of laughter with what seem to be the most ordinary of remarks afterwards.

Max Miller's 'Well . . .' or 'No I don't, not me lady . . .' are what might be termed charismatic triggers for prolonged humorous outbursts. Laughter itself, like thought, springs from inscrutable origins and blessed indeed are those who would tap them for us.

At a distinctly less humorous level, we might now look for a moment at mass fright and panic. Here, we could take up Elias Canetti's terminology, in his classic book *Crowds and Power*, and refer to *Flight Crowds*. He maintains that this particular type of crowd is the most comprehensive:

> It contains absolutely everybody and the picture of diversity which it thus presents is further complicated by the differing speeds of the fugitives: there are young and old among them, strong and weak, those less and those more burdened. But the picture is misleading. Its motley colours are only incidental and, measured against the overpowering force of direction, utterly insignificant.

The basic, raw, animal emotion of flight consumes all. The very word 'panic' derives from the God Pan and implies something of a supernatural drive which instils fear of being destroyed by some stronger and awesome foe. Panic sets in when the direction of flight is impeded and man fights man as the mass emotion of near hysteria grips all. Is it possible to advance any further in theoretical terms and profitably to speculate as to how the emotion of fear is generated and transmitted?

Obviously the autonomic nervous system is involved, so that there are gross changes in the rates of heartbeats and breathing and perhaps in digestive or even excretory processes; the human body reverts to its animal prototype as the body prepares and adjusts itself to flight. There would doubtless be external stimuli in terms of physical disturbances (volcanic eruptions, attacks by armed troops, earthquakes) causing all to surge in common movement; yet, this spreading of mass fear may involve other factors besides the momentum of being caught up in a mass movement or a flight from danger towards the goal of safety.

Such a mechanism may be connected with the macrophages, which are defined by Heine in his book *The Vital Sense* (1960) as 'the reticule endothelial system of amoeboid cells' which are to be found under the skin of the body and connected with the nervous system. In any extremely emotionally charged situation the following process takes place:

> Factors of this kind (i.e. stress) would stimulate the macrophages strongly, and would cause the free nerve endings to transmit messages of stress to the hypothalmus, which would then proceed to sort them out and to act upon them by stimulating the pituitary gland, which would thereupon release secretions which would lead to an increased output of thyroid or adrenal or gonadal hormones.

The chemical communication system is thus activated, as is the entire nervous system; it is possible that these body changes are capable of being transmitted to others, perhaps by some sense of taste or smell. There are references to the 'smell' of fear, and there are many sensitives who experience variations of taste and smell when confronting others. Freud imagined that telepathy was an ancient method of communication, perhaps accompanied by chemical changes in bodies.

Thus, in 'flight crowds', and perhaps in other mass gatherings, chemical changes are stimulated which are capable of being transmitted and contagion sets in. Certainly the autonomic nervous system is excited unduly, and there are heightened states of great emotion which spread rapidly. The actual pressing together of bodies may further facilitate such emotional transmission, as in the case of a tightly packed football crowd behind the goal contrasted with the more staidly seated members in the stands. One of the proposed solutions to crowd violence is an expansion of seated accomodation, and there would thus seem to be theoretical reasons for such a measure.

It is in the crowd that mass emotions become heightened as individual experiences of being isolated from others physically are temporarily excluded. Elias Canetti maintains that the elimination of the fear of being touched by others – going back to animal days of combat perhaps – is a prime feature of a dense crowd:

It is only in a crowd that man can become free of this fear of being touched . . . the man pressed against him is the same as himself. He feels him as he feels himself. Suddenly it is as though everything were happening in one and the same body. This is perhaps one of the reasons why a crowd seeks to close in on itself: it wants to rid each individual as completely as possible of the fear of being touched.

Complete invulnerability thus being experienced on the physical level, the emotions play more fiercely and sweep through crowds like waves across the waters of a lake. Emile Durkheim, the French sociologist, spoke of 'emotional currents in crowds' and most of us have experienced the surge of mutual feeling, whether it be in support of a football team or a pop star.

But how are emotions transmitted? Here, again, we are into the realms of the metaphysical. In his book, *The Science of the Emotions* (1924) the Indian writer, Pandit Bhagavan Das, after observing that emotions tend to create their own likeness, described the process of emotional transmission thus:

> Each thought and emotion sets up its own rate of vibration in the inner bodies. This vibration, travelling outwards, tends to set other inner bodies, which it contacts, vibrating at the same rate . . .

Thus are we back to Mrs. Garrett's 'magnetic field' which she thought to be the medium of telepathic projection. Yet in crowds, even though there might be some subtle vibrating of as yet unidentifiable energy bodies, there are sights, and even smells and sounds which might arouse common passions: Canetti draws attention to the unity of emotions in the baiting or flight crowds, and these draw a common emotional stimulation from outside cues, be they seen or heard. The severed head of the executed criminal, for example, used to bring an instant roar from a crowd, as does the scoring of a goal on the Kop at Liverpool. Simultaneous sensory reaction to a common focused stimulus may thus be mistaken for emotion transmitted in some occult fashion.

As a boy, Le Bon, the author of *The Crowd* (1909), had been a keen student of the French Revolution and absorbed many accounts of the years when the mob seemed to rule and aristocratic heads rolled. In fact, at all points the crowd were subtly directed by other aristocrats or intellectuals, who saw the newly awakened democracy as a tool for their own political ends. It is recorded that the King's cousin, the Duke of Orléans, who helped to usurp the monarch, concealed himself in a pillbox on the Champs-Elysées, green foliage in his hair crying '*A bas les aristos!*' with several of his followers at strategic points *en route* to the Bastille echoing such anarchic sentiments. It is important to keep the momentum of hate going; focus the venom of the crowd on an object, a person, or a group of persons and they will act. Thus with the object of destroying the Bastille (which they took to pieces, stone by stone), their rulers and the underpinning aristocrats, the crowd became incensed to a degree rarely seen before in history.

Passionate opinions, then, are a necessity for crowd unity. These may be connected with almost anything; they may be true, false, ludicrous or plausible. All that is needed is emotional fervour, As Hoffer writes in *The True Believer*:

> It goes without saying that the fanatic is convinced that the cause he holds on to is monolithic and eternal – a rock of ages, till his sense of security is derived from his passionate attachment and not from the excellence of his cause. The fanatic is not really a stickler to principle. He embraces a cause not primarily because of its justness and holiness but because of his desperate need for something to hold on. Often, indeed, it is his need for passionate attachment which turns every cause he embraces into a holy cause.

Among adoloscents, in particular, there is a need for passionate attachment, and such demonstrations as the adulation of the Beatles in the Sixties and the rejection of authority by campus students at the University of Berkeley revolted by the Vietnam War – these indicate the unifying action of a passionate focus. The individual becomes submerged in collective feelings, and these must relate to the very core of one's being to be affected. Paul Goodman, of the Beat generation writing in 1960, makes an interesting point about the appreciation of foot-tapping jazz (thin gruel) as opposed to the gut-appeal of pop-music, more exciting in its volume and rhythm. In the dark of today's disco the lights and blaring jungle sounds may disquiet adults: but for the emotional young there is the rich inward feeling of group unity and a communion with older and more satisfying deeps which go back to less urbanized days. In the blare of rock music, indeed, is an ancient appeal.

In crowd behaviour, then, the individual becomes lost or fulfilled, depending upon the perspective taken. Outside stimuli at sight and sound levels excite and inspire, emotive oratory – preferably dealing with future, glorious and only generally-specified states – may inflame, and the need for movement and sound is generated yet again. Now these last two often take on typically ryhthmic features, and such mass accoustic and reverberating patterns somehow emphasize all the excitement, glory, hope and wonder which radiates – certainly at sensory levels – and may extend to other energy fields marginally outside the physical.

All too soon, however, the crowd disperses and the carnival, metaphorically speaking, is over.

Perhaps the last word in this chapter might go to Elias Canetti, of Spanish Jewish origin, who was in his thirties in Vienna when Hitler was in power and would have had opportunities of studying crowds and power: mercifully, he left to settle in England in 1938 and his seminal work on collective behaviour was published in 1960. He hints at the subtle alchemy of physical and emotional desires when he writes:

> Only together can men free themselves from their burdens of distance; and this, precisely, is what happens in a crowd, During the discharge distinctions are thrown off and all feel *equal*. In that density, where there is scarcely any space between, and body presses against body, each man is as near the other as he is to himself; and an immense feeling of relief ensues. It is for the sake of this blessed moment, when no one is greater or better than another, that people become a crowd.

7

Thought-directed

An important element in the very word telepathy, meaning the action of thoughts or feelings being directed by an agent and received by a percipient at a distance, involves the dynamic process of sending such abstracts forth, and it seems appropriate that a chapter should be devoted to a closer examination of cases where there appear to have been willed efforts to convey ideas or physical and emotional conditions. (The hypothesis that there actually *is* a willed sending forth has not gone unchallenged in the past in some quarters: the French scholars of parapsychology, Richet and Sudre, would prefer to use 'metagnomy', or shared knowledge. By so doing emphasis may be placed upon receivers as well as senders – too often the latter are given the limelight at the expense of the former.)

One of the best-documented sources of willed thought-direction is Gurney's *Phantasms of the Living* which was mentioned in Part I, Chapter 2. The 1300 closely filled pages covering 700 cases recorded in some detail are monuments to the industry of Myers, Podmore and Gurney. Compiling such a work must have taken up much of their spare time for many years, and they saw it as a positive demonstration that perhaps humans were more than mere flesh and blood and that some greater world of spirit brooded nearby. Their data refer to the living projecting themselves into the presence of others, often in times of crisis or illness. Some of the most remarkable cases, as has been mentioned earlier, are those involving the appearance of somebody thought to be living but suddenly appearing at the very moment of their death before a relative or close friend. It may be argued – but never proved, of course – that some last thoughts were concerned with being in the presence of certain others, and the three instances below indicate the possibility of thought-direction at the time of death:

Case 557   6 November 1884
When I was about 10 or 12 years old, I was sitting one evening, towards dusk, at the piano practising, when I saw an old lady, the grandmother of one of my schoolfellows, enter the room. I was in the habit of seeing her frequently, and recognized her perfectly. She was very old, and to the best of my belief had never entered our house at all, so that I was greatly surprised to see her. I heard the next day that she had died on the evening I saw her. I never had any other hallucination.

Case 564
... I was startled at seeing my dear old friend from Sevenoaks pass the window, and go towards the front door ... on opening the front door there was no one to be seen ... I afterwards learnt that at that hour my friend died. ...

Case 567   October 1884
... On Thursday I retired to rest at about 10 o'clock when, on looking at the foot of the bed, I saw my mother standing dressed in white; her features were very distinct. I spoke to my husband and asked him to look at the foot of the bed, as mother stood looking at me. He said, 'I don't see her; can you see her now?' My reply was, 'Yes.' After that she vanished slowly away . . . the next day we had a letter to say my dear mother was at rest. I can still see her as plain as at that time. The date was November 1846. I have never had another vision but this one.

SARAH AMOS

And, tellingly, there is the observation from the author that 'We find from the obituaries in two Dover papers that Mrs. Amos's mother, Mrs. Wilson, died on November 21st, 1846'.

Since then there have been many accounts of thought-bodies, or astral-doubles, being projected into the presence of others. The botanist Robert Crookall has listed over 1500 cases in this century, and contemporary study groups usually refer to such phenomena as OOBEs (Out-of-the-body experiences).

One of the most explicit statements as to the nature of this directed double was given by the eminent journalist and psychical researcher W.T. Stead, who was to perish on the R.M.S. *Titanic* in 1912. In a book published in 1891, entitled *Real Ghost Stories*, he instances four ladies 'between twenty and forty years of age' from whom he received 'first-hand accounts of bodily duplication'. One of his informants, a Mrs. Wedgwood, who was related to Charles Darwin, is thus described by Stead on such an occasion:

> She was lying on a couch in an upper room one wintry morning at Shorncliffe, when she felt her Thought Body leave her and, passing through the window, alight on snowy ground. She was distinctly conscious both in her material body and its immaterial counterpart. She lay on the couch watching the movement of the second self, which at the same moment felt the snow cold under its feet. The second self met a labourer and spoke to him. He replied as if somewhat scared. The second self walked down the road and entered an officer's hut, which was standing empty. She noted the number of guns.

After reuniting the two bodies, Mrs. Wedgwood went down to breakfast and described to the company where she had been and what she had seen. One officer corroborated the numbers and types of guns.

W.T. Stead, after commenting upon the worthlessness of such a statement in terms of evidential value, makes a significant point about such accounts:

> They may be worth as much as the confessions of witches who swore they were dancing with Satan . . . but any explanation of subjective hallucination or of downright lying would be preferred by the majority of people to the acceptance of the simple accuracy of these statements.

Public attitudes have not changed much in a century.

Stead questioned another woman as to the nature of the thought-body and received the following reply:

> It is difficult to explain truths on the plane of thought to those

who are immersed body and soul in matter. I can only tell you that every person has, in addition to this natural body of flesh, bones and blood, a Thought Body, the exact counterpart in every respect of this material frame. It is contained within the material body, as air is contained in the lungs and in the blood. It is of finer matter than the gross matter of our outward body. It is capable of motion with the rapidity of thought. The laws of space and time do not exist for the mind, and the Thought Envelope of which we are speaking moves with the swiftness of the mind.

'Then when your Thought Body appears?'

'My mind goes with it. I see, I hear, and my consciousness is with my Thought Envelope'.

But then the idea of ingrained dualism, of a spirit within a body, is as ancient as recorded history. It is only within the last century or so, in fact with the rise of industrial society, that the belief has been seriously challenged.

Perhaps for the remainder of this chapter it might be best to dwell on efforts made when the thought-body works within or with its conventional physical structure. But it might be said that we are still in the field of the miraculous and unexplainable, even when we raise our little finger. Where, in fact, does the ability to muster the effort of will to do so come from? Is it physiological in origin or are more obscure variables involved?

The will, recognized by the Greeks as a specific area for study and cultivation, receives only general attention from psychologists. Yet in the field of telepathy it may play an important part, according to those theorists who see the process as dynamic. The first adventures of the Creery sisters in 1880, which were to spearhead Barrett's data on thought-transference two years later, neatly suggest the ideal willing conditions for success in telepathic experiments. It will doubtless be noted that such are not generally cultivated in the pitiless and long-drawn sessions involving drawings and card guessing, and that they involve a certain type of orientation, or willed interest in the proceedings. I quote this time from Myer's account who, in turn, gives the actual words spoken by his friend, the Rev. A.M.

Creery, in whose household the events first occurred in October 1880. He is describing the early trials involving his young daughters and a maid-servant to whom they were much attached.

> Each went out of the room in turn, while I and others fixed on some object which the absent one was to name on returning to the room.
>
> After a few trials the successes preponderated so much over the failures that we were all convinced there was something very wonderful coming under our notice.
>
> Night after night, for several months, we spent an hour or two each evening in varying the conditions of the experiments, and choosing new subjects for thought-transference. We began by selecting the simplest objects in the room; then chose the names of towns, names of people, dates, cards out of a pack, lines from different poems, in fact any things or ideas that those present could keep steadily before their minds; and when the children were in good humour, and excited by the wonderful nature of their successful guessing, they very seldom made a mistake. I have seen seventeen cards, chosen by myself, named right in succession, without any mistake.

And now comes the all-important reference in any telepathy experiments to the matter of directed thought:

> We soon found that a great deal depended on the steadiness with which the ideas were kept before the minds of 'the thinkers' and *upon the energy with which they willed the ideas to pass*. Our worst experiments before strangers have invariably been when the company was dull and undemonstrative; and we are all convinced that when mistakes are made the fault rests, for the most part, with the thinkers, rather than with the thought readers.

The italics in the above passage are mine, for they connect with the only psychic experience I have ever personally known. The incident, curiously, links with ideas of a thought-double, and also the energy behind willed ideas.

I was on holiday with my wife and children at the home of one of my writer friends in Jersey. One Saturday morning I borrowed his brake to journey to St. Helier, which was perhaps half a dozen miles away. I was given strict instructions by all to be back for midday, at which time we were to go to another friend's house for lunchtime drinks. I parked the vehicle in a car park in St. Helier and carried out a few shopping chores and the usual enjoyable visit to an antiquarian book-shop where I lingered. On coming out I realized midday was half an hour away and went in search of the car park. Incredible though it may seem, I could not find it. The idea of actually failing to find a car park must seem ridiculous to many (it had not happened before to me and has not since) but there were several such small ones in St. Helier and it took me perhaps an hour before I finally found it after a long process of trial and error and using a map. During my roamings midday came and went, and I could imagine the party waiting in some irritation for me as my frustration mounted. On arriving back at my friend's house, I was met by his wife. She had waited alone for me, the others having gone on in other vehicles.

'Why did you go away again?' she asked. I said I hadn't been back.

'Harry heard you drive through the gate. He was by the pool.' (The pool was raised on a terrace above.) 'He looked down over the wall and saw you get out of the brake, go to the back, open a door and take a box out. Then he came down to talk to you and you'd gone.' My friend had been the only to see me, and, when I rejoined the party, expressed amazement when I said I hadn't been back to the house. To this day I think he believes that I drove in about twenty minutes before midday – when my frustration at not finding the car park was perhaps at its height – and he has frequently repeated his story about it.

If I am to accept the idea of the phantasms from Gurney's book then some part of me, unknown to my conscious being, not only projected a shade of my being back to the house, but also a shade of the brake and the box of books I was apparently taking from the boot of the car. To this day I can only grope for an explanation, but on reading through Creery's account of the early thought-transference sessions, I can more keenly ap-preciate the phrase relating to the importance of energy willing ideas.

A further, somewhat strange, stepping-stone might be the
grandstand of an abandoned racecourse on the outskirts of
Berlin in August 1914, where H. Desmond Thorp was interned
for the war years with other Britons. He published a remarkable
book on his adventures, mostly mental, when he returned home,
entitled *Etheric Vision*. At the beginning of his enforced
detention, he was a young, well-educated business man, something of a *bon viveur*, and dismayed at being confined to the same
narrow environment indefinitely. Something of the flavour of
this comes across in the early stages of his book:

> Before my internment, the natural appeal of the big town to a
> comparatively young man had not left me with much time for
> concentrated study. What with dance parties and week-end
> trips and my usual occupation, the time for serious study
> seemed ever lacking . . . but now I had time in plenty . . . for
> weeks and months on end I read as much as six to eight hours
> a day. There, on the dusty seats of the old grandstand I would
> sit pouring over abstruse volumes, stopping every now and
> again to rest my eyes as I gazed out of the vault of
> unobstructed skyline overhanging to the one-time fash-
> ionable race-course. In this manner, the habit of sober
> reflection and meditation formed on me and 'brown studies'
> became the order of the day. . . .

His idea to branch out in a novel direction came from reading a
book whose title had been forgotten – it was one by Rudolf
Steiner of Theosophical leanings – and suggested that the best
laboratory for assessing the reality of psychic phenomena was
'God's great out-of-doors'. Thorp was also lucky in finding an
immediate, limited and infinitely testable hypothesis (replicable
also by all and at many times today). He stated it as follows:
'that it was possible, given a background of clear skyline,
unobstructed by clouds or fog, by means of the naked eye alone,
to see the atoms of space'. For our purposes, an additional phrase
might be added to the effect that it is possible by the willed
direction of human thought to cause these small light particles to
form patterns, thus suggesting that thought, after all, may be
manifestly transmittable.

Thorp was at first doubtful about the idea. 'I admit that it was with some misgivings that I undertook the task at all, and I anathematized myself as a credulous fool at the outset', he confesses in the early part of his book, but, after about only half an hour of staring into the blue sky one day, he found himself gazing upon *thousands of shooting emanations* which seemed to occupy the whole of space and were in 'pulsating perpetual motion'. At this stage, of course, it is possible to say that Thorp had become disorientated in some way, perhaps through solitude and boredom, or perhaps through his internee's diet. 'Spots before the eyes' is a common enough complaint, after all. However, the author is adamant; anybody, with perseverance and practice, may perceive these swirling patterns of specks on any day when the sky is clear and blue. He also believes that they have something in common with meteorites in that they flash, sparkle and fade, and suggests that they issue from some potent parent source. He also echoed ghostly ideas of Mesmer when he wrote:

> It would appear indeed that the whole of space is full of this 'matter in being', one might call it, which acts as a sort of dam holding back the life principle within, and that this space matter collects in nuclei not unlike a sponge, through the pores of which a little of that potential energy escapes from time to time in the form of an electric charge, and thus energy is transmitted through space and transmuted into matter *ad infinitum.*

Heady metaphysical speculation indeed, but, when Thorp again exerted the force of his thoughts and will, even more bizarre words and ideas were offered. He felt that these light particles were in some way 'linked up with some hidden or latent potential in man' and sought to demonstrate this to himself.

The first occasion when his thought appeared to manifest he states to have been in the summer of 1917, when he would have completed almost three years of internment. He writes that his nervous and physical condition was depleted, and critics in favour of a hallucinatory hypothesis seem to be in a strong position indeed. He first tried, by thought concentration, to stop one of these light particles in its tracks. The passage below, in which he succeeded in doing this, is one of the most theoretically significant in the postulation of an all-important psychic atmosphere linking man and space (as guessed by Mesmer, Reichenbach and Lodge) or it is yet another anecdote in the doleful literature describing mirage or hallucination under physical and mental privation. After exerting a strong effort accompanied by a cry of 'Halt!', Thorp wrote:

> There it stood for about fifteen seconds and would not or could not budge. Though all these details happened in a much shorter time than it has taken to describe them, the mental strain combined with the shock of the surprise was excessive. I could hold out no longer; the command was rescinded, the tension relaxed, and the next moment that little lambent spheroid sped on its way to join its fellows in the great unknown. My elation at this further success knew no bounds, and I sprang to my feet and began to dance about like a man possessed.

He carried out even more amazing experiments: willing 'eons' to move left or right, up or down, forming letters of the alphabet ('. . . there it stood, glittering and twinkling, a gorgeously beautiful jewelled 'A' suspended in space . . .') and finally, after being released into Holland, conjuring up the face of his deceased mother in the blue space of the sky. In his book he also records his silent dialogues with The Voice (which he attributes to his subconscious mind) which pointed out the possible subjective nature of the exercise and thus the 'intellectual cul-de-sac' that this presented.

I have not been able to trace any further reference to Thorp. Certainly the opportunities for replication by all are immense, like Rolf Alexander's inconclusive experiments in making clouds disappear. (Some of us at College in the 1950s were attracted to such research; as one student wryly observed, supine in the hot Worcester sun on a green playing-field and in congenial company, the whole area of investigation calls for really sustained efforts over long periods.)

Although Thorp, his Berlin racecourse grandstand, and his eons may be roughly consigned by critics, to sad imaginings it is less easy to do so with the experiments of Mlle. Tomczyk and Dr. Ochorowitz at the Polish University of Lemberg in 1911, as reported by the lawyer Nandor Fodor in his book *These Mysterious People* (1934). It seems a curious feature of the literature in parapsychology that such rich data should often be condensed in non-scholarly publications. The photograph of suspended scissors, for example, appeared in *The Bristol Evening World* in 1934 and seems to have been generally ignored in ensuing mountains of commentaries on matters psychic, Dr. Ochorowitz was a most distinguished Polish psychologist, and Mlle. Tomczyk one of his patients whom he had hypnotized for therapeutic purposes. Fodor writes:

> She could stop a clock by looking at it. She could produce movement in objects without contact. She could influence a roulette to the extent that the number chosen by the medium turned up more often than justified by chance.

Such statements are both interesting and provocative – if only Fodor had given finer details of the events mentioned above and, especially, the experimental situation. Critical materialists may often be accused of inhibiting a sensitive's performance, but they are at least alive to possible ambiguities in reporting and also to the way in which an experimental situation of research pattern may bias results. We need 'the hygiene of research', as the educationalist Wiseman once wrote or, to echo him, we must be 'squeaky clean' to quote the zoologist Jeremy Cherfas, a contemporary, energetic and conscientious researcher into the human condition.

The photograph reproduced on p. 120 depicts a pair of scissors raised from the table. Mlle. Tomczyk is exerting her will, and Ochorowitz furnished us with a psychic/physical explanation. He maintained that fine threads or invisible rigid rays emanated from the finger tips of the medium and were the means by which the scissors were enveloped and raised. These threads could be cut but were immediately formed again. 'It seems formed of points', he wrote. 'It can be photographed and it is then seen to be much thinner than an ordinary thread. It starts from the fingers. Needless to remark, that the hands of the medium were carefully examined before every experiment'.

Other mediums, such as Mme. d'Esperance, Margery of Boston and Frau Ideler, have all spun such threads by thought

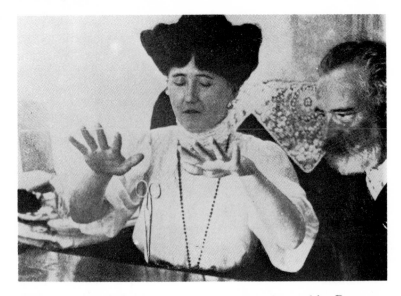

Mlle. Tomczyk wills a pair of scissors to rise, observed by Dr. Ochorowitz, a lecturer in psychology at the University of Lemberg in Poland (1911)

to facilitate psychokinetic phenomena. The astounding conclusion thus emerges from these data that willed thought is capable of moving objects. (Given the climate of our times, however, it seems unlikely that this idea will be given credibility or that replicatory experiments will be made.)

Support for the implicit hypothesis of Myers that in telepathy there is a movement of thought from the agent to the percipient thus gains ground a little. If thought can be directed towards objects, as evidenced by telekinesis, then the popular idea of thought rays going from one mind to another (or one surround and via this to the brain) is not so far out after all.

Thought-photography, the willed direction of ideas on to a sensitive plate, enjoys more acceptance than Mlle. Tomczyk's raised scissors or faltering roulette wheels. The many experiments carried out by Dr. Eisenbud on the medium Ted Serios are comparatively well known, and demonstrate that an idea clearly visualized in the mind's eye may be transmitted to a negative and thus printed. Hans Holzer, among others, has pioneered psychic photography, being mainly concerned with manifestations of the departed. However, in his book on the subject in 1976, he has this to say on the matter of ectoplasm, that effluvia from a medium which builds up into faces or bodies of the dead:

> This material, isolated some years ago in London and found to be a moist, smelly whitish substance related to albumen, undoubtedly comes from the body glands of the medium and her sitters or helpers. It is later returned to the sources, or that portion of it not used up at the end of a seance. It can be moulded like wax into any form or shape. *Strange as this may sound, it is thought direction that does the moulding.*

The italics are mine. According to Holzer, thought-direction must often be discarnate, since mediums are often in a state of deep trance when ectoplasm emanates from their bodies and shapes form. The rather startling possibility thus emerges that the dead can will thought into visible forms, rather like some sky pilot trailing white words of some advertising slogan. In the photograph on page 122 two young soldiers, Lieutenants Naylor and McKenzie, apparently manifest after death through two mediums; critics may suggest that such photographs are faked but reasons for mediums to indulge in such heartless activities seem obscure.

An outstanding example of the dead using ectoplasm to appear and also to pass on an opinion (implicitly in this case) is one quoted by Felicia Scatcherd in her 1926 booklet entitled *Ectoplasm*. She was looking for rooms with a friend in the Russell Square area of London, and her companion was tired and 'sitting on a high chair so that her mantle hung in long folds to the ground'. Presently a mass of globular ectoplasm began to form beside her and:

> out of it looked a living face, normal in size – a man's face with rolling eyes and a leering grin that made one's blood run cold. When I mentally ordered him away he grinned defiance. Fearing to startle my friend, I took the landlady aside and asked what was the matter, She burst into tears.
> 'Oh miss! Did you not see him? He was my first. He's come

Thought forms of the war dead: Lieutenant McKenzie (*left*) and Lieutenant Naylor (*below*) If genuine, these photographs suggest that ectoplasm from the medium may be moulded into human likenesses by mediums or discarnate entities

like this several times, and has never forgiven me for marrying
again . . . you must have seen his wicked face glaring at us
from your friend's cloak and now you will not take the rooms!'

It is of interest here that Miss Scatcherd actually transmitted a
thought to the materialized head and was, spontaneously it is to
be supposed, rebuffed. Again, we are in the sad situation of an
extremely significant event not being followed up, and, for that
reason, likely to be rejected by the more adamant materialists.

A notably scholarly, and equally neglected work involving
the thought-direction of ectoplasm from the living and the dead
(at least in theoretical terms), is the second of two volumes on
the Goligher Circle (so-called from the name of three of the
group of mediums) by the mechanical engineer W.J. Crawford.
The first was *The Reality of Psychic Phenomena* which gave
singularly exact details of such matters as the levitation of tables
by ectoplasmic rods and the weight loss of mediums before and
after sittings. In the second, published posthumously after the
suicide of the author (caused by overwork and not, as malicious
critics have suggested, to his disillusionment with ectoplasmic
phenomena), David Gow, editor of the spiritualist magazine
Light, in which successive accounts of the Goligher Circle had
appeared, had this to say of the author, a scientist:

> For the rest, I may pay tribute to the careful, courageous and
> most valuable work of the departed scientist, in an obscure
> but tremendously important branch of scientific research.

The book was published very shortly after the First World War,
and is illustrated by several photographs showing ectoplasm
extruding from a medium's body, building up into rods, and
causing a table to tilt. There are also many diagrams indicating
the play of mechanical and gravitational forces, and the whole
work is reminiscent of some volume on physics rather than one
akin to the amorphous literature of the seance room. The
photographs shown here illustrate how ectoplasm issues from
the body and finally, it is claimed, forms a rod 'stronger than
iron' to tilt the table. The part played by thought in bringing
about such movements is, of course, extraordinarily complex,
more so as the general idea of ectoplasm and its capability of

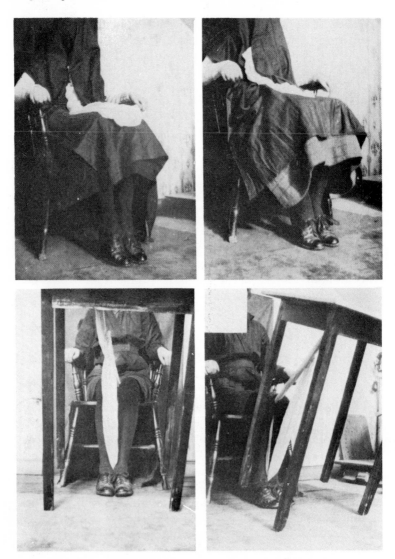

Thought directed: the Goligher Circle move a table with ectoplasm
Many would consider these four photographs faked, but
spiritualists claim they are genuine and illustrate how ectoplasm
may be moulded by the thought from discarnate entities

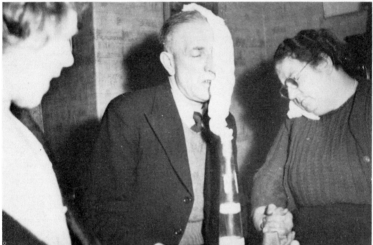

Photos of ectoplasm taken at private sittings in Bradford in the 1940s

moving objects is largely disbelieved in the 1980s.

The intention of the Circle was to move a table and to photograph the process. Members of the group were the Goligher sisters, Lily, Kathleen and Anna, their young brother and two or three others. Sessions were held in Ireland between 1917 and 1919 but, as Crawford writes, 'The elucidation of the mysteries of the psychic structures at the Goligher Circle took several years to work out. The work was difficult, troublesome and laborious'.

One thought component thus came from the sitters, but Miss Kathleen Goligher, the principal medium, would go into a deep trance and give vocal instructions to the rest while in this state. These came from a group called 'the operators' who would give Crawford innumerable opportunities for inspecting the mechanism by which ectoplasm might be directed by their thought to levitate a table.

In the past, ideas of thought-direction, ectoplasmic extrusions, psychic photography and phantasms have understandably smacked of the bizarre and otherwordly; there is something faintly neurotic – a retreat from reality – in concerning oneself with such nebulous areas. Yet knowledge, the goal of psychic no less than physical science, should positively contribute towards the well-being of humans, and it is towards this area of directed-thought that we may now turn; to the area of healing others by psychic endeavours, which legitimately comes within the scope of telepathic study.

8

Healing

Although telepathy is associated in the public mind with thought-transmission and scientific testing, the capability some people have of causing healing influences to pass into another being is legitimately within the field of the transference of states of feeling; the very word 'dis-ease' reflects how we feel, and there is now a mass of accumulated evidence which suggests that states of health in humans may be induced by others. In this chapter we shall be dealing with the positive and beneficial instances of such a process, although there are many, particularly in non-industrialized societies, who believe that malefic influences can cause ill-health, or even death, from a distance. As with other manifestations of telepathic phenomena, we await theories and causal explanations. Those who are healers claim variously to be the agents of God, or of those who have gone before (after the school of thought which we might attribute to the spiritualist/naturalist Russell Wallace), and others claim a view more consonant with the ideas of Tom Lethbridge (see page 188ff) – that we have an energy nimbus which may beneficially react with those being healed. The bedside manner of the doctor, perhaps, reflects the commonsense notion of the benefit given by a soothing presence.

Let us first look at typical cases in order to assess whether cures were temporary or permanent. As was seen in the chapters on crowds and hypnotism, some people are extremely suggestible in a public situation, and the throwing away of sticks and the straightening of limbs on the healer's platform are commonplace. What is less well publicized is whether such apparently miraculous cures are permanent. Dr. Lawrence Leshan, an American psychologist who has spent years investigating psychic healing, believes many so-called cures involve only temporary relief, and that in perhaps as many as 90 per cent of cases there is regression to the earlier diseased state. Thus, he maintains, arguments using cases of genuine cures become weakened by the majority of reported temporary 'cures'.

The only objective evidence for evaluating such supposed healing would be by considering photographs taken before and after the treatment. The following example is taken from *Supersenses* by Charles Panati, in my view, one of many books published in the 1970s which blend case histories and imaginative theory well, but which do not seem to have achieved much recognition at an academic level outside America. The occasion was a group healing session in New York, where 'several hundred people shout the name of Jesus while scores more kneel in fervent prayer'. Panati writes:

> In the case of the woman suffering from acute arthritis, X-rays taken of her hands on days following treatment revealed a steady and substantial decrease of the knotty calcium deposits in her bones. By the week's end, the X-rays showed not a trace of calcium overlay.

Leshan has considered many cases of genuine healing and states that the healers themselves, notably in non-Western countries, are almost unanimous in saying that they are agencies for some outside external force which works through them. To obtain the best results, they feel the need to be tranquil emotionally and physically, losing themselves to become possessed by some spirit agency. Yet another school of thought, he says, is that a healer awakes within a patient some sort of self-repair process, which has lain dormant. Other medical psychologists believe that there is some sort of 'energy flow' from healer to patient which helps or supplements this repairing capacity. It is interesting that these two theories are in line with telepathy transmission ideas: say, the ideas of the nature of the subconscious, as propounded by Osgood Mason, Fellow of the New York Academy of Medicine, and others in America at the turn of the century (see page 169), as opposed to those of Sinnett and others who would subscribe to the 'energy flow' idea. It is also thought by Adamenko, a Russian physicist, that the flow fruitfully stimulates acupuncture points.

What do the healers themselves have to say about the healing process? Is it a personal matter, or do healers draw upon some great Unknown Power, whether it be known as the subconscious mind or various deities?

We might first look at some eastern experiences, Yogi Ramacharaka wrote a book entitled *Psychic Healing*, published in Chicago in 1906, which gives a useful outline of oriental belief systems concerning various energy fields unacknowledged by westerners. He writes:

> He is taught from childhood that there are many subtle forces and forms of energy in Nature, which may be taken advantage of and pressed into service by Man. To the Oriental there is as much mystery and awe about electricity as about psychic force – in fact, he sees them as but varying forms of the same thing and he respects them both . . . healers are but channels of expression through which the natural forces and energies flow.

One such force he terms 'Prana', the name given by the Yogi philosophers to the vital force or energy which is found within the body of every living thing. It may be called the Life Force. He maintains it is mental in nature and, rather obscurely but nevertheless in line with others who consider thought origins, is the 'Energy of the Mind of the Universe'. Prana, he suggests, may be transmitted from one person to another by making passes over the sick person or by the age-old method of 'laying on of hands'. He instances cases from ancient Egypt and China where carvings and other illustrations depict this process. Hadrian is said to have cured people having 'dropsical diseases' by applying the points of his fingers to them, and the early kings of both England and France healed goitre and throat diseases by 'the King's touch'. Pranic healing is thus of ancient origin and is practised by healers the world over.

A recent example from the USA is quoted by Panati in his book. He writes of Ethel De Loach of New Jersey, whose powers have been studied by scientists for five years, and who came to psychic healing when her daughter was kicked on the knee by a horse. No doctor was available and the girl was in considerable pain, whereupon her mother tried laying her hands on the injured part and felt her hands 'taken over' as the pain subsided.

Since then she has healed many people, often of obstinate illnesses, and she uses the acupuncture points as a reference for her healing.

Kirlian photography (a recent technique of photographing electrical energy streaming from the body), of course, endorses that there is some vital flow, notably at the fingertips. This process has received much controversial publicity, but there is no doubt that the fingertips of a person in good health present a different, and vigorously 'bushy' picture from those of one physically depleted. Further, it may serve to give tangible evidence of affinities or dislikes between people. Dr. Thelma Moss, one of the first American scientists to observe Kirlian photography during a trip to Russia in 1970, comments in Panati's book:

> In some cases the energy fields attract each other, and in other cases they push each other away – just like a magnet. My guess is this is why some people like each other instinctively when shaking hands. You can call it good vibes and bad vibes.

Endorsement of the 'energy field' school of thought in healing between people comes from Dr. Dolores Krieger of New York. She has been practising the 'laying on of hands' for several years and maintains that healing forces may be transmitted from one person to another and that 'anybody can do it who has the desire to heal'.

These optimistic American statements are made in good faith and no doubt based on much evidence, notably from those who are eager to help. We have already seen that telepathy tests in general are affected by the very factors that make much of psychic healing possible: motivation, good health, and a certain relaxation and absence of tension. However, the ability to produce test results above the mean is rare, and it may be that in the population as a whole effective healers (notably those who can bring about permanent cures) are rarities.

One such singular person is Dora Van Gelder, born in Java of Dutch parents, who sees auric surrounds in much the same manner as other psychics mentioned earlier in this book. In the parapsychologist Hammond's book, *The Search for Psychic Power*, she is quoted as being able to differentiate between various layers of this elusive surround, which is mentioned so often in the literature of psychic healing, and also to outline its working mechanism. Hammond quotes her thus:

> I can see the energy fields which flow through your body – there's the physical field, which tells me about your physical condition. Then there's the mental field, which tells me what you're thinking, and the emotional field, which shows what you're feeling. The emotional field sticks out about eighteen inches from your body and is more like a kaleidoscope, a changing colour pattern. I can walk down the street and know in a split second if a person is disturbed or normal.

Here, indeed, at a sweep, is a comprehensive explanation of how sensitives may see disease, and some theoretical framework for an explanation of telepathy. She goes on to discuss auric mechanisms: 'This energy field flows through the organs of the body in a stream-like motion. When I see blockages, or breaks, in the field, I know this indicates a disease process.' She uses Indian terminology to describe seven *chakras*, or wheels in the human body, which link with the glands and help to circulate the energy flow referred to above.

Obviously the whole area cries out for corroboration since if people could develop powers of diagnosing disease visually, then the cure rates would escalate. However, Dora Van Gelder, came from a family which practised meditation and studied eastern religion; her grandmother and mother were both psychic, and she was guided in psychic studies in Australia by an Anglican priest who was himself a psychic. Further, now in her seventies, she has been a non-smoker and teetotaller all her life, and is a vegetarian. She is thus a well-disciplined human being, and rather removed from the ordinary everyday world. Most of us, the vast majority, are ordinary folk; we are to be counted with Richet and Sudre, the French researchers who would sit looking patiently and fruitlessly at glass Kilner screens, filled with purple dye, in an endeavour to see the illuminating human colours observed by such psychics as Mrs. Van Gelder. The road towards the development of such superhuman sight seems a long one, with few of us sufficiently sensitive to use such frames of reference.

There seem to be few accumulated statistics as to whether cures have been permanent or temporary, and diseases cured (or uncured) by healers have not been classified. Hospitals are chary of allowing healers to come into wards, although there have been occasional exceptions. Medical opinion is cautious, rightly pointing out that auto-suggestion is ever a potent factor in recovery. Furthermore, faith healers may alleviate pains which, in themselves, are symptoms of serious diseases. Thus temporary 'healing' may have fatal results. Certainly the training of medical students is as conventional as ever, and there is not a whisper of matters psychic in the curricula of medical schools; it is considered odd to show any real interest in the occult, this particular branch of human studies being outside the present paradigms of medical science. This, of course, contrasts with such opinions as those of the scientist Franz Alexander and the astronomer Sir James Jeans. The latter is well known as observing that 'the universe begins to look more like a great thought than a great machine' and the former, along with many other intellectuals, bemoans the myopia of scientists as well as doctors.

It is perhaps indicative of the trend for telepathy pioneers to become interested in psychic healing that J.B. Rhine recently associated himself with the Foundation for Research on the Nature of Man (a high sounding title indeed) in Durham, North Carolina. In one experiment mice were anaesthetized in pairs and healers concentrated upon selected specimens, attempting to bring them back to consciousness. 'We found that the mouse under the direct influence of the healers woke up sooner than the other mouse. This experiment was repeated many times with different healers and different mice' commented the veteran of telepathy research. It would be interesting, yet ethically undesirable, perhaps, to repeat this experiment using humans. In the Twenties Vasiliev in Russia and others experimented successfully in sending humans to sleep from a distance (see page 175), and thus the influence of a conscious mind upon another *is* demonstrable.

As always, the reason moves hesitatingly towards some sort of framework or explanation and, apart from the rather misty area of auras and energy fields whose presence is undetected by all but a very few, there are few real advances. Too often the explainers become lost in a fog of physical theories involving matter, energy, the movement of molecules, and other difficult-to-grasp concepts. It seems that the faith of the recipients is not a crucial variable, be they agnostic, atheist or believer. Many enthusiasts attend healing services and their symptoms are not relieved, while others, agnostics, are cured spontaneously. Some healers make use of spirit guides (often, it is alleged, deceased doctors); others believe in energy flows referred to earlier, while others suggest a physically beneficial interaction between themselves and the sick persons.

It is hard to imagine that there is one overall explanation. Certainly in many instances the healer feels depleted after a session. In one of Matthew Manning's cases (he now elects to concentrate upon healing – see page 182ff.) he spent three days with a Norwegian in the last stages of terminal cancer in order to relieve him of almost unbearable pain. 'For a week after his death I could feel all these aches and pains inside,' he remarked some time afterwards. 'It was as if the pain had somehow been transferred to me – or perhaps it was a kind of telepathic sympathy between us'. This also links up with the common phenomenon of husbands experiencing the labour pains of their wives, and those with close sympathetic bonds (mother/daughter notably) simultaneously experiencing distress when one or other is injured.

From the vast mass of literature on psychic healing it is obvious that here, indeed, is another area ripe for sustained research, since benefits are immediate and of great human importance. Half the hospital beds in the UK are filled by those suffering from non-physical ailments, and it is possible that fit people, perhaps acting in groups, could help. Yet conventions and altruism are at odds, for willing though many people may be to help in some way, medical institutions are chary of organizing such an enterprise, which is likely to be many years away. A massive recording of successes and failures of faith healing, whether lasting or temporary, is needed; as long as accounts are fragmented and remain outside the field of conventional medicine the general status of faith healers, however well-meaning, will remain questionable.

9

Cards, names and numbers

Card guessing and telepathy often go together in the public mind. A conventional image of rigorous test conditions perhaps contains one person willing to another some card design or denomination, accompanied by impressive statistical analysis involving computers; and it is generally vaguely supposed that such procedures may lead up to some great findings one day.

Half a century of such activity hardly supports the hope. Rhine in the USA and Soal in England have been among those who placed faith in such methods, and there are hundreds of accounts of their experiments and methods. Inconclusive findings and a multiplicity of methods have, of course, provided much rich ammunition for those opposed to the apparent whimsicalities of psychical research. Early criticisms, such as the receiver being able to see designs through thin cards, unconscious choice patterns of senders perceived by receivers, and occasional trickery, have been raised again and again by more recent critics.

Parapsychologists have thus sought academic prestige in their associations. The famous establishment at Duke University in North Carolina was originally sponsored by the psychologist William McDougall, a much respected figure; armed with his status in psychology he was able to place the young J.B. Rhine (then recently converted to such matters by a lecture given by Conan Doyle) in charge of 'a search for Faculty X', as Colin Wilson, the writer, might have put it. In his penetrating book *Mysteries*, he points out that will-power and experimental rigour form only a small part of experimentation, and that surrounding variables such as relaxed, sympathetic and unhurried procedures are also important. The academic card guessers, however, placed their faith in rigorous laboratory conditions and the reporting of such tests in publications or at meetings of the highest academic standing; for, in science, the academic status of scientific explanations is all important, whether it be in the case of the Piltdown man, evolution, or even Marxist or establishment analyses in the social sciences.

In 1947, S.G. Soal was invited to be the speaker at the prestigious annual Society for Psychical Research Myers lecture and in 1950 J.B. Rhine was the memorial lecturer. By the late 1940s the activities of Rhine and Soal were thought to be of prime importance in psychic circles, the principle subject investigated being telepathy, and their main methods of detecting such an elusive phenomenon revolving around card guessing experiments; usually they experimented with all the trappings of physical science rituals in terms of laboratory settings, minutiae of recording and, particularly, remorseless statistical analysis of the mountains of results which accumulated down the years. Soal, in particular, being a mathematician, wrote endlessly on measures of significance in terms of expected and observed frequencies of successful as against unsuccessful guesses. In his book *Modern Experiments in Telepathy*, written with Bateman and brought out in 1954, Soal devotes some forty pages of appendices to dealing with various modes of statistical analysis, featuring such concepts as target lists, chi-squareds, decline effects and deviations. He ends his book with Appendix J entitled 'W.L. Stevens' Method of Evaluation', which begins thus:

> Suppose that a pack of N cards contains k different sorts of symbol which we shall refer to as 1, 2, 3 . . . . . k. Let there be a_1 cards of the first symbol, a_2 of the second, etc. up to a_k cards of the last or k^{th} symbol. Suppose that k symbols are guessed, g_1, g_2 etc. up to g_k times, so that clearly,
> $$N = a_1 + a_2 + \ldots \ldots a_k + g_1 + g_2 + \ldots \ldots g_k$$
> Then, provided that N cards are adequately shuffled, the expected number of successes or 'hits' on the N guesses will, if chance only is operating, be given by:
> $$E = \frac{1}{N} \sum_{v=1}^{k} a_r g_r$$

No doubt statisticians would take in W.L. Stevens' method at a glance, but most non-mathematicians would quail and may regretfully assume that to be a telepathy investigator a fair knowledge of statistics is called for. In fact, the rigour of Soal's statistical treatment reflects, as much as anything, the need felt at the time for psychical research to be seen to be scientific and, therefore, to be taken seriously. (It is obviously useful to know something of statistics if card guesses are being recorded; but there is one cheerful school which maintains that statistics, if they are significant at a spectacularly casual level, will shout; getting 20 cards right out of 25 when only around five are expected is obviously well beyond chance, for example, without any formulas needed. Marginal significances are more likely to apply to the fine experiments of physical science within a laboratory, rather than some hopeful human science equivalent.)

The title of Soal's address was 'The Experimental Situation in Psychical Research' and in the first few words of the published version of his address, the speaker nailed his colours to the mast:

> I have chosen an experimental topic, since for the past two years I have been doing card-guessing experiments with Mrs. Gloria Stewart of Richmond, Surrey. And nowadays the cobbler is always expected to stick to his last.

As he warmed to his topic, Soal observed: 'Let us turn now to what is probably the most promising method of investigating paranormal cognition. I refer to card guessing.'

He went on to write about the experiments of Coover and others early in the century and dates the famous Zener cards, with their five 'geometrical symbols' (circle, star, cross, oblong and waves), from 1932. He mentions the massive accumulation of the 100,000 card guessing trials of Rhine. Unwittingly, he suggests reasons for his own rigorously scientific approach in one part of his lecture:

> There is unfortunately among American investigators an atmosphere of showmanship which has created in the minds of British scholars a deep distrust. British scientists for instance are not favourably impressed by Rhine's discovery of

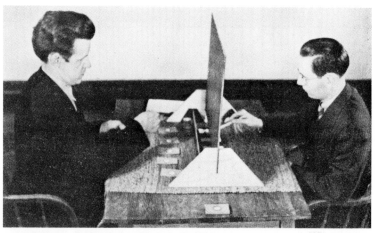

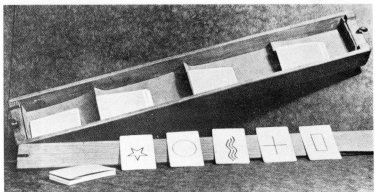

Photographs showing the use of Zener cards at Duke University, illustrating the rigour of laboratory experimental work (1932)

a telepathic horse (or was it a precognitive pony?), by the sudden vanishing of Dr. Reiss' phantom percipient into the blue of the Middle West, by the perfect scores of 25 cards correct in 25 successive guesses alleged to have been made by Pearce and the child Lilian, by the card guessing feats of Pearce while sitting in a motor car, and similar marvels.

Perhaps it is worthwhile quoting this last incident of the test in the car in some detail, for I think it not unimportant in methodological terms. What seems to me a detailed account is given by Rhine in his book *New Frontiers of the Mind* (1937). Alas, the guessing was done by one Linzmayer, not Pearce. I do not wish to criticize Soal, for we all make errors – and one of the tricks of any researcher is making the best of fallible humans in seeing that they are not too discouraged when, as must happen from time to time, they are mistaken in statement or calculation. Better still, checking systems should operate which help us to produce more accurate observations and figurings. Rhine's account runs thus:

> Linzmayer had a theory that he could do his best if he made his runs while looking out of the window. He thought this slight diversion kept him from getting fixed mental habits about calling the order of the cards . . . I suggested going for a ride in my car to give him a chance of attention. My plan was to stop after a time in some quiet place and do another test or two. Then we could go on to another, and a third, as long as the method seemed effective . . . I pulled the car up at the side of the road but did not bother to turn off the engine. Putting a large notebook across Linzmayer's knees, I took a pack of ESP cards out of my pocket and held it in my hand. He, meantime, had leaned back with his head resting against the top of the seat, so that his eyes saw nothing but the roof of the car. There were no mirrors or shiny surfaces into which he could have looked for possible reflections. During the actual progress of the test, his eyes were closed.
>
> After giving the pack a cut – neither of us knew the order of the cards in it anyway – I drew off the top one and tipped it towards me just enough to catch a glimpse of the symbol and then put it face down on the notebook on Linzmayer's lap. Without looking at it or touching it he said, after a pause of about two seconds:
> 'Circle'.
> 'Right,' I told him, drew off the next card, and laid it on the notebook.
> 'Plus,' he said.
> 'Right'.
> 'Waves'.
> 'Right'.

'Waves'.

'Right'. At this point I shuffled the pack again, cut it once more, and again drew off a card.

'Star,' Linzmayer said when the card was placed on the notebook. It was a star.

When he had called *fifteen cards in succession* without a single mistake, both of us were too amazed for a while to go on with the rest of the run. . . .

The odds against the 15 successive accurate calls being due to chance are 30,000 million or so to 1. Such a performance, as Rhine comments, is virtually impossible by all rules in the book of chance.

It is at this point, of course, that critics have a field day. How may we be sure that Rhine was telling the truth? What of the test conditions – they certainly weren't rigorous, and Linzmayer would only have needed the merest glance from the corner of his eye to have seen the card selected by the man seated beside him.

One can counter at an apparently unscientific level, invoking the convenient goddess of Intuition: the story has a ring of truth about it somewhere – and Linzmayer was subjected to all manner of laboratory tests in which his scores varied from the exceptionally exceptional to the ordinary. Conventionally, fatigue and boredom lowered scores. It seems that, all in all, he was unusually receptive.

There are other high scorers: Hubert Pearce called 25 cards in succession correctly, the odds against this being 298,023,223,876,953,125 to 1. On that occasion Rhine held the cards, which were returned to the pack and a cut was made each time. Pearce had come in, not intending to make any tests, and stood there in his overcoat. Rhine was in a joking, challenging mood, and kept up a banter about betting sums of money on the cards being called. At the end of the run, concluded at twenty-five by some odd mutual consent, Pearce commented 'Well, you'll never get me to do that again'.

He never did.

So Rhine became a celebrity. For forty years he conducted research at Duke University, introducing his famous dice experiments where students concentrated on certain numbers appearing – one wonders why subsequent fieldwork could not be carried out to financial advantage at Las Vegas and other places. He founded *The Journal of Parapsychology*, and his wife Louisa Rhine became a distinguished lady in the field of ESP. He came to London to the SPR in Tavistock Square, to give the Myers Memorial lecture in 1950. Soal introduced him, and with these words hinted at a shift in opinion on the importance of card guessing in telepathy research:

> What would he [Myers] have thought of the card guessing and picture guessing experiments that figure so prominently in modern research? I think he would have recognized the value of these methods in the impression they make on scientific opinion, but he would have been quick to realize that by their very nature they cannot take us much beyond the threshold of the subject. Card guessing, he would probably have said, is too crude and feeble an instrument to throw much light on the telepathic process itself – and I think he would have been right.

The eminent Rhine (then 55,) held forth on telepathic ESP and clairvoyant ESP and paid a generous tribute to the 'really striking results' obtained by Soal on Basil Shackleton and Mrs. Stewart. ('You will, of course, ignore all the Shackleton stuff,' remarked one distinguished SPR scholar to me a year ago. He belonged to the school of critics headed by Professor Hansel, who published *ESP – A Scientific Evaluation* in 1966 and criticized Soal and Rhine at all levels, concluding that 'a great deal of time, effort and money has been expended but an acceptable demonstration of the existence of extra-sensory perception has not been given'.)

By the 1980s card-guessing experiments have become fewer in terms of on-going research. It is generally recognized by modern researchers, such as Carl Sargent at Cambridge, that a more relaxed attitude is needed and that percipients, particularly, should only take part in such experiments when they feel their mood to be right. Indeed, Soal in his book on experiments in telepathy put the matter in a nutshell, in spite of his over-enthusiasm for statistical niceties:

Telepathy and the unconscious
Depth psychologist C.G. Jung (1875–1961) (*left*) suggested that
J.B. Rhine (*right*) and his fellow workers never properly
appreciated 'the far-reaching conclusions that must be drawn from
their findings' in relation to the subconscious mind

> It is among those who cultivate intuition and feeling rather
> than intellect that we should prosecute our enquiries . . . to
> function well, the sensitive needs freedom from distraction
> and the presence of friendly people who are prepared to
> adapt themselves to his mental idiosyncracies.

Card guessing is a useful method of discerning whether
individuals have telepathic powers, although the informality or
otherwise of the occasions may have an influence on scores.
Rhine obtained his best results in the case of his spontaneous
card readings with Pearce and Linzmayer; in the 1870s the
Creery girls and their friend the young servant were at their
most effective when in a happy mood and before the researchers
arrived; and Soal's most successful tests were with two Welsh
cousins, both called Jones, in 1956 and 1957 done out of doors
and in informal situations. Critics would point out that these last
two groups tried to cheat on occasions, but this often happens in

the case of both mind-readers and mediums if they have to work over long periods and experience poor results at times.

Perhaps, as a result of the monotony card guessing, other pictorial devices, involving the reproduction of many different kinds of drawings, were gradually introduced, as will be considered in the next chapter.

10

Reproducing drawings

Telepathy enthusiasts, at least in their early days, are often attracted towards the idea of attempting to receive drawings from a distance; the Zener cards, with their repetitive rigidities of design, sometimes lead to boredom or a feeling that little knowledge about telepathy is going to accrue from such activities. With drawings there seems to be a richer range of expressed mental activities, and successes may be more easily depicted, and even more effectively publicized, as evidence of the coincidences of mental visualization. 'I'm from Missouri – show me!' is a sceptical aphorism attributed to the late President Truman, but the idea of producing evidence goes back a long way in the history of conversions: impressive, independent accumulated evidence must win the day, missionaries always imagine, and the early investigators in telepathy may have felt the same way about their drawing enterprises.

In the much-quoted classic *Phantasms of the Living*, Gurney and his collaborators describe in some detail the experiments of October 1883 involving the reproduction of drawings by telepathic means.

'We owe these remarkable experiments to the sagacity and energy of Mr. Malcolm Guthrie, JP of Liverpool,' wrote Gurney. 'At the beginning of 1883, Mr Guthrie happened to read an article on thought-transference in a magazine, and though completely sceptical, he determined to make some trials on his own account'. A clearer statement of scientific research directed by the null hypothesis (H_0), much publicized by the philosopher Karl Popper and others in recent years, could hardly be put. Guthrie began by assuming the proposition to be false and let evidence build up and tell its own story. Later in the year he wrote:

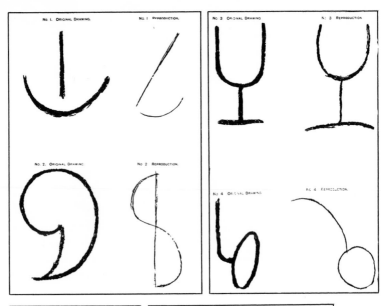

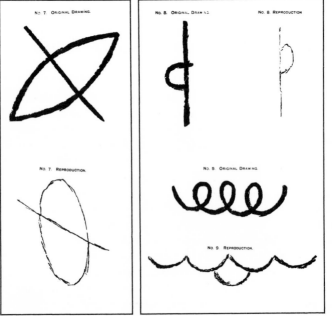

Drawings transmitted telepathically
Some examples taken from *SPR Proceedings*

It is difficult to classify them. A great number of them are decided successes; another large number give part of the drawing: others exhibit the general idea, and others again manifest a kind of composition of form. Others, such as the drawings of flowers, have been described and named, but have been too difficult to draw.

He goes on to say that there are variations in performances, successes coming quickly and in runs and being followed by failures, as may be expected if human attention and the onset of fatigue are factors that matter. Both he and Gurney go into considerable detail as to the probity of the experimenters, whose names give an interesting sample of the social backgrounds of psychical researchers of Victorian times; Birchall and Steel, respectively secretary and president of the Liverpool Literary and Philosophical Society, Guthrie the JP, and Hughes and Gurney, scholars from Cambridge. 'The names of the percipients were Miss Relph and Miss Edwards,' added Gurney, not feeling the need to give any backgrounds, let alone deal in detail with the research attitudes of two such important parties in the experiment. But, in those early days, the emphasis appears to be upon the power of the agent rather than the psychology of the percipients.

The eight illustrations on page 144, representing the series of drawings in consecutive order at a single sitting between Mr. Guthrie and Miss Edwards are remarkable by any standards of evidence. A fair conclusion from them would be that it is possible, under some circumstances, for one person to perceive drawings in the mind of another. There are also manifest opportunities for replication of these experiments, and also variations in terms of percipients trying to discern drawings without agents (clairvoyance) and interactions between friends, relatives, non sympathetics, males and males, males and females, and other permutations.

Particularly interesting are the comments of the young 32-year-old Oliver Lodge, then the first professor of physics at the newly formed Liverpool University; they more than make up for any lack of information on the ladies mentioned above:

With regard to the feelings of the percipients when receiving an impression, they seem to have some sort of consciousness of the action of other minds on them; and once or twice, when not so conscious, have complained that there seemed to be no 'power' or anything acting, and that they not only received no impression, but did not feel as if they were going to.

I asked one of them what she felt when impressions were coming freely, and she said she felt a sort of influence or thrill. They both say that several objects appear to them sometimes, but that one among them persistently occurs, and they have a feeling when they fix once upon one that it is the right one.

One serious failure depresses them, and after a success others follow. It is because of these rather delicate psychological conditions that one cannot press the variations of an experiment as far as one would do if dealing with inert and more dependable matter, though in some cases a stranger has proved a good agent straight off. . . .

Again, research opportunities, which have rarely been followed up and the advent of which has been frowned on by established science, are suggested by this sensitive and insightful commentary. The initial 'thrill' may indicate that the nerves and brain are alerted before pictures are formed in the mind's eye, so that the nervous system itself must be a primary focus in any explanation of the telepathic process; and the ever-present need for sympathy and encouragement in such experiments is clearly stated – in all human interactions, of course, such variables, sadly often overlooked, often determine the quality of rapport, notably in the links between young and old. In the more formal relationships of commerce or soldiering, for example, it would seem that such empathies are not necessary for the efficient carrying out of the prescribed processes; yet others would argue that true leaders lead from the heart, and that the expressive dimension underpins the instrumental. Certainly in the telepathic experiment of the transmission and perception of drawings it seems that these early experiments produced evidence of a truth which may well apply to other exchanges.

The experiments at Liverpool in the reproduction of drawings at a distance bore little fruit, however. There were numerous replications, more or less successful, but few speculations as to theory. In 1906, the American investigator James

Hyslop, formerly professor of ethics and logic at Columbia University, reproduced the Guthrie drawings in his book *Enigmas in Psychical Research*. The extreme caution which even he, a believer, urges, largely in response to the critical attitudes of the times, may be gleaned from the following:

> Experiments of this sort continued during the first eleven years of the Society's work, and extended reports of them were made. Critics and sceptics must go to its *Proceedings* for the measure of their value, and not treat the examples here as scientific proof of telepathy. I can only illustrate the type of phenomenon which lay claim to that interpretation, and such as have reason to believe the trustworthiness of the experimenters and their conditions will be impressed with such as I have quoted.

Hyslop conducted another type of experiment which, although not concerned with the actual reproduction of drawings on paper, relates to the inducement of pictorial matter in one mind's eye by another. In the course of these experiments, consideration was give to what might be a decisive factor in their success, that of participators being in the same room or apart. Hyslop's research consisted of agents transmitting objects or pictures and percipients attempting to visualize these. He carried out experiments involving such images as sailing boats, kittens and banjos, and he commented upon his results as follows:

> Where the agent and percipient were not in the same room there were but two successes out of fifty-five trials; where the agent and percipient *were* in the same room, there were thirty-one successes out of seventy-five trials. It requires no statistician to deduce the significance of such findings.

Thus, right at the beginning of the twentieth century, an important clue was thrown up which might be considered when generating a theory as to how the telepathic process takes place: for the greater the number of successes when participators were in the same room, suggests some link which may be strengthened by proximity, or by making actual physical contact.

The Smith and Blackburn experiments mentioned in Part One, Chapter 2 give another example. These were conducted in 1882 by Gurney and Myers, Douglas Blackburn being an SPR member and G.A. Smith a young mesmerist. Although Blackburn suggested some thirty years later that there had been trickery, it is hard to read the following careful report, written in 1882, without considering the possibility that trickery alternated with genuine phenomena (as in the cases of the Creery sisters and the Jones cousins tested by Soal). There is also the strong suggestion that physical distance or contact between the percipient and agent may be a factor of importance:

Next day (December 4) we varied this experiment, thus:
One of us, completely out of sight of S., drew some figure at random, the figure being of such a character that its shape could not be easily conveyed in words; this was done in order to meet the assumption that some code – such as the Morse alphabet – was used by S. and B. The figure drawn by us was then shown to B. for a few moments, – S. being seated all the time with his back to us and blindfolded, in a distant part of the same room, and subsequently in an adjoining room.
B. looked at the figure drawn; then held S.'s hand for a while; then released it. *After being released*, S. (who *remained* blindfolded) drew the impression of a figure which he had received. It was generally about as like the original as a child's blindfold drawing of a pig is like a pig; that is to say, it was a scrawl, but recognizable as intended to represent the original figure. In no case was there the smallest possibility that S. could have seen the original figure; and in no case did B. touch S., even in the slightest manner, while the figure was being drawn.

As the twentieth century has progressed, more evidence has accumulated as to the reality of drawings being reproduced by telepathic means. The American socialist and author, Upton Sinclair, developed strong drawing links with his wife, which he explained by using the phrase 'mental radio', reflecting acceptable telepathic models for the times (the 1930s). Again, as in the case of Guthrie, he began with the null hypothesis.

One of the most persistent experimenters in the use of

drawings to demonstrate telepathy was Whateley Carington, a Cambridge scholar in Edwardian England and leading light of the SPR in the 1930s and 1940s. After his death in 1949, some 20,000 drawings were left behind from his endless experiments. Rosalind Heywood, eminent and aristocratic medium who sat with him during some of these tests, has an interesting reminiscence of the man in her book *The Infinite Hive*, albeit *post mortem*:

> At the old headquarters of the SPR in Tavistock Square, I used to meet an invisible man wandering about the small room at the back of the stairs and the passage which led to it. He seemed to be in a state of acute anxiety.

She mentions that two other sensitives were conscious of the impression of some sort of presence, and one of them positively identified the researcher: '. . . a pale thin man with hollow cheeks and wispy grey hair' was the description, similar to the appearance of Carington as Rosalind Heywood had known him. She continues:

> A year or two later I wanted to look through the records of the experiments I had done for Carington and asked the secretary of the SPR where they were stored. 'Here,' she replied, 'with all his experiments. They are on the shelves behind the curtain just inside the little back room'.

Some idea of the tensions and frustrations that he suffered, in common with those who persist in repetitive scientific activities with only a small group of helpers, may be gleaned from a passage in his last, almost completed book, entitled *Matter, Mind and Meaning*:

> Often enough, wearied with my efforts and dissatisfied with their results, I came to a stop, and the field is filled with cognita describable as forebodings of failure ever to get this book finished or make people understand what I am trying to explain, accompanied by those unpleasant sensations mainly of visceral origin (sinking feelings) with which all who are liable to depression are only too familiar.

Yet for all his persistence with a limited number of experimental methods, often involving the reproduction of drawings, Carington made many interesting points, as a perusal of *SPR Proceedings* relating to his work reveal: he established that drawings *could* be communicated, he rediscovered the displacement effect, whereby a past or future drawing might be reproduced – although this has always been notoriously disputed, for runs of drawings conspicuously concurring with past or future runs need to be emphatically produced – and, perhaps influenced by the Fascist rallies of the 1920s and 1930s, he put forward the importance of group influences upon individual minds.

Certainly he drew attention to the poignancy of the isolated researcher and writer; there has ever been the need for cooperation and an exchange of views among all psychic investigators, no matter whether they be classified as artists, scientists, poets or merely interested; indeed, 'merely interested' strikes a faintly disparaging note, for it is often the interested amateur who sparks off research work carried out institutionally. In matters psychic, individual experiences are of very great importance.

Moving to more modern times, the American investigators Russell Targ and Harold Puthoff of the SRI (Stanford Research Institute) carried out 'remote viewing' experiments in which a 'target team' would go out to some location and concentrate upon a landmark or country scene, and a subject in a laboratory some distance away would note down any feelings or connections – and also make drawings. Targ and Puthoff have described successes, but the psychologists Marks and Kamman of New Zealand's Otago University have drawn attention to the need for no cues to be given beforehand, and they comment that 'any target can be matched by any description to some degree'. (Perhaps such modern experimenters should look back to the work of Guthrie and Hyslop, who showed, clearly, that physical proximity between agent and percipient is more likely to lead to results than any distant ponderings upon country scenes or buildings!) Yet the interest and energy shown by the American and New Zealand research teams are welcome. Targ and Puthoff have not only produced a mass of absorbing data down the years, and the New Zealand psychologists introduce a welcome note of caution. Interestingly, the Americans, both physicists, have suggested that psychic abilities can be learned, as shown in the case of young metal benders.

The topic of metal bending became popularized in the early 1970s by Uri Geller and others, and Professor John Hasted, with his definitive book *The Metal Benders*, clearly demonstrates unequivocally the proved existence of such a phenomenon. In this work he also gives details of telepathic tests involving drawings between young metal benders, Geller and Hasted and his family. There are obvious correspondences, as shown on page 22, almost as vivid as the work of Guthrie a hundred years before, and it seems that those who deny that drawings may be reproduced by psychic means are more misinformed than prejudiced.

Over the last century, however, the repeated efforts of researchers to convert sceptics have been generally unsuccessful. It may be that more liberal and encouraging attitudes are coming in, as evidenced by the New Zealand psychologists Marks and Kamman, who only recognized the need to study parapsychology when pressure from their psychology students forced them to do so.

The long history of sending pictures by the mind, and the mountain of data accumulated, once again points out the need for theory and practice to go hand in hand. Prevailing knowledge systems and conventional social constructions of both and physical and psychical reality are always at the back of research projects, to say nothing of the sensitive matter of research funds and facilities being provided or not. Hence, as in the case of Lodge and Hyslop, on-going experiments should link with theoretical speculation, for without theory practice is myopic; and without practice, theory is uninformed. Such a tag, borrowed from the philosophy of science, should be kept in mind by all those who would undertake visualization experimental work in the area of telepathy.

11

Telepathy and time

Studies of time and telepathy reveal many interesting features about our beings, for some abstract sector of us does not relate to time. We may reach a physical peak in our mid-twenties and thereafter begin bodily decline, but any industrious academic will avow that there is little comparison between his mental powers at twenty and fifty, for various works of scholarship attest to the superiority of the latter age. There are other aspects of our nature which also actually improve with age: we generally become more patient, tolerant and methodical; the wonder of nature, the beauty of friendship, appreciation of the arts and sciences, and the enjoyment of music - time brings us keener aesthetic pleasure. And those three watchdogs of intellectual health, namely interest, an unhurried approach, and systematic method often mature down our physically declining years. We may be trapped bodily in time and space as we travel our million or more miles round the sun, spinning madly the while, but there is a finer mental side to our beings which is somehow outside the senses, and it is in this strange area that thought seems often not tied to time at all .

The eternity of the happy fleeting moment is a common experience. We have all felt those moments of pleasure when we have wished for time to stand still. On the other hand, time passes all too slowly when pleasure or interest is lacking. And, of course, in our everyday thinking we can please ourselves whether we consider the past, present or future. Our minds, unlike our bodies, may not be timebound.

It is indeed strange that some can, or claim they can, perceive the past or future thoughts of others, but these odd interactions seem dwarfed by premonitions of future events, which have been copiously recorded under the parapsychological heading of precognition and come from occult origins. Here might we weave odd imaginings of awesome presences, beyond us, in some elevated position above the factory floor of our everyday life, watching the process by which the machinery of time and place warps and wefts the textures of biographical patterns. Perchance at times such entities are able to warn us of approaching designs that we may modify these.

Let us consider examples from telepathy research where time-slips, either backwards or forwards, have been noted. These occasions have often occurred unexpectedly and as a kind of byproduct to the main experiments being conducted. It is part of the belief system of science in general, of course, that the true gold mined by tedious research lies in the unexpected event or discovery, as in the case of Fleming's penicillin or Archimedes realizing the significance of his displaced bath water. There is always thus some faint justification for proceeding with the most tedious and prolonged research procedures, in the Micawberish hope of something odd turning up somehow somewhere. In few fields of laboratory endeavour is such patience called for from investigators in particular as in telepathy testing with cards, drawings and objects. Those three stalwarts of telepathy research, Messrs. Rhine, Carington and Soal, are probably the doyens of a community of patient scientists. Their carefully recorded testings, largely carried out in the Long Weekend between the wars, during the 1920s and 1930s, seem inspired by the wish to show that man is more than his five senses and entrapped in time and space. Were any unexpected golden coins minted in their experiments? I would certainly put Rhine's personal experiences with Pearce and Linzmayer as examples of strikingly odd successes, and unplanned at that; and in the cases of the two British investigators, their work during that period contained one or two interesting tangential features, which we shall now examine, especially as they relate to telepathic experiences outside the normal sequence of simultaneous visualizations or impressions between agents and percipients.

The first incident concerns the zealous Dr. S.G. Soal, whose calculations as to probabilities in telepathy testing have (dare I say probably!) never been bettered. In the mid 1920s the wireless had come into use, and the Society for Psychical Research was quick to persuade the BBC that here indeed was a

Heaven-sent opportunity for carrying out telepathy experiments between accredited SPR agents in the studio and interested listeners. In 1927 and 1928 the first experiments included attempts 'to broadcast telepathic impressions of objects shown to agents for a period of three minutes each'. Sir Oliver Lodge was the announcer, and a staggering 24,659 replies were received from listeners. Only some 150 obtained 'partial successes', which is in itself an interesting indication of the rare capacity for sensitive telepathic perception. Critics, of course, would point to coincidence, and interested readers are referred to Soal's extensive work on expected frequencies of success in these experiments, where some significance, in spite of the small numbers of only 1 in 164 or so being remotely successful, is demonstrated.

These 150 apparently sensitive persons were invited to take part in further experiments, involving transmissions on Wednesdays between 8.30 and 9.00p.m., 10 minutes being devoted to individual experiments. Soal considered a way in which the agents in the studio could be physically activated, perhaps thus enhancing their transmission powers to listeners at their sets and crystals. He wrote:

> My intention was to make preparations for a little chemical experiment to startle the agents during the last ten minutes of the half hour. On the morning of 5 October I carried to town in my attaché case, a small bottle of sulphuric acid, a glass rod and a packet containing a mixture of sugar and potassium chlorate. I was intending to make a small white pyramid of this mixture and to place it on a tray in the seance room. While the agents were watching I would suddenly let fall a single drop of the concentrated acid on to the mixture from the end of the glass rod. There would have been a spluttering, crackling conflagration, rising almost to the ceiling, and acrid fumes of chlorine peroxide would fill the room as well as smoke. . . .

Understandably, Soal had second thoughts and decided to abandon the project at midday thinking that 'the smoke might damage the ceiling'. He purchased instead 'a large toy rabbit with long ears, brilliant scarlet back and white woolly breast' which was duly and silently transmitted by Soal and two others from 8.50 to 9.00 p.m.

The accounts of the agents seem straightforward enough; the responses from percipients were carefully recorded and appear in detail in two hundred pages of *SPR Proceedings* Vol. XI from 1931 to 1932. From this mass of detail Soal notes the following response from percipient No. 28 (there were 58 percipients altogether) who alone actually picked up thoughts which had occupied Soal's mind earlier in the day. He wrote in as follows: 'Something crackling or spluttering as water dropped on to acid. Irritating fumes. Idea of ammonia.' No. 28 wrote later that he had nothing to do with chemistry and that 'the impression was the most sudden and unexpected of any I have as yet received'.

Yet another occurrence of the unexpected is one concerning Soal and his associate Mrs. Fernald. On 2 November 1927 percipient No. 20 had written in response to an experiment involving the transmission of objects and drawings after 8 p.m. on that evening: 'Something being lighted that would give a bad smell. A dazzling light. A bad smell again: perhaps an explosion. A hissing or gas-escaping sound.' Before the session started, Mrs. Fernald had been deputed that most human of tasks, making coffee. After seeing the response from No. 20 she mentioned to Soal an incident which had occurred earlier and which he subsequently recorded thus:

> Between 7 and 8 p.m. J.H.F. [Mrs. Fernald] twice let the gas escape while making coffee. The second time the tap was turned on for several minutes before the gas was discovered to be unlighted, and filling the room. We all exclaimed 'there might have been an explosion'.

Again, as in Soal's cancelled experiment in chemical combustion, there is the strange link between a relatively tense occurrence and its reproduction at a future time and at a distance; again, some hypothesis that there is some intermediate medium upon which the event was impressed, stored and perceived might be put forward, so that a return is made yet again to the rather whimsical theoretical field of auras or human atmospheres to use Dr. Kilner's terminology.

What might be fairly deduced from these two unexpected events, and their reportings, which occurred at the edges of the rather intense business of systematic experimentation? I suggest the following speculations:

1. The notions of the possibility of the chemical experiment, and the 'near-miss' of a gas explosion, came into the conscious minds of Soal and Mrs. Fernald and were then, perhaps, relegated to a subconscious area where, nevertheless, an impression of their emotional connotations still lingered. We are all aware of similar instances in our own lives, and the way in which such incidents often surface later in dreams. It is as if the experiences are rather like vegetables in an Irish stewpot, which are dropped in and come bubbling to the surface in sleep or later conscious recollections.

2. At a later stage, within a few hours in both cases, percipients had mental, physical and emotional impressions of these occurrences. This idea of a percipient being able to recall an agent's feelings as well as images, both immediate and anticipatory, are features of other communications mentioned throughout this book. In everyday life, of course, as in the chapter on wartime experiences, these 'recollections' often occurred simultaneously with the experience of the agent. Here, perhaps, lies a fruitful prescription for future research.

3. Although these two cases point to the possibility of telepathic communications, telepathy is shown to be very much an exceptional occurrence. To give an example, on 10 October 1928, 414 percipients were sent the picture of 'red artificial poppies' (one would have thought this somewhere in the minds of percipients with the Armistice Day Anniversary but a month away) yet nobody mentioned 'artificial red poppies'. One person described poppies, 37 flowers of some kind, and 30 red objects. Radio telepathic links are thus obscure and it is difficult to compare the results of sending such mental pictures with chance occurrences.

4. The uncomfortable realization thus appears that possibly millions of thoughts and impressions are in some state of ethereality or limbo, for the most part ignored but, possibly, unwittingly picked up on occasions. Parallels between a myriad of radio signals selectively received by approximately tuned sets loom irrestibly: but the telepathy signals, unlike the radio waves, appear to exist timelessly and also know no space limitations.

Unexpected results in experiments at least go some way to establishing positively the existence of telepathic communication, and also generate interesting speculations as to the nature of the process of sending and reception. But, as Richet and others have pointed out, the hypothesis of the message *travelling* is unproven: if, say, a green traffic light were to show in a street in Birmingham at the same time as one in Bournemouth, there would be a coincidence of manifestation; hence two thoughts of the same nature in two minds at the same time – or at different times – does not necessarily mean that a flow of some sort has taken place. A synchronicity of impression only has occurred.

From the very detailed account of the broadcasts, and the follow-up experiments introduced by Julian Huxley from October 1928 to March 1929, it is possible to gauge the enthusiasm of Soal and his helpers; the researcher produced many tables; and his graphs of probability calculations are perhaps without parallel in the history of telepathy experiments. With the development of mass media, replications might profitably be carried out and the beyond-chance results obtained by Soal could be reproduced. However, the motivation to organize such a massive enterprise may well be lacking, as was not the case in the Twenties when the novelty of broadcasting held out romantic hopes for epoch-making experiments. All that was really achieved was slightly more than random successes being registered; and the mechanism of telepathy remained as inscrutable as ever.

Indeed, zealous and prolonged experiment has usually been preferred to theoretical speculation down the years. However, someone who did not shrink either from mental rumination or putting forward bold and abstract theories was Charles Mace, an educationalist and the author of a very useful book on the technique of study still in use today. In 1937 he delivered the Frederic Myers Lecture at the SPR on the subject 'Supernormal Faculty and the Structure of the Mind' in which he touched upon the evidence for telepathy; if this is accepted, he suggested, then there must be a causal connection since coincidence is ruled out:

> To deny coincidence is to assert causal connection. The two possibilities are alternative and disjunctive. It cannot be both and it cannot be neither. If it is not a coincidence the connection is causal, there is no third alternative.

But what sort of causal mechanism does he suggest, where thought may be transmitted from past and future sources, as well as the present? We might therefore look, in terms of stimulus and response, for a framework outside our usual ideas of sound, heat, light and radio transmissions. Mace later put forward what Mesmer, Sinnett and others had stated before him, a conclusion which was italicized in the report of the lecture: 'We are led to postulate some non-physical substance upon which the stimulus acts and within which or to which the effect event occurs'. He criticized the relatively crude idea of some 'psychic ether' on which events are impressed and later recalled. However, he recognized the need for a new explanatory concept of retention and firmly stated:

> Personally I am of the opinion that we can, with a good scientific conscience, postulate the existence of a medium which records impressions of all sorts of events, and which later or elsewhere may produce a corresponding pattern.

He ended his address with the rather forlorn hope that here was a matter for co-operative research between psychologists and students of psychical research, but almost fifty years after his lecture little progress has been made, and the two camps of which he was a member are still poles apart.

There is one chance remark Soal records which may be of relevance to Mace's ideas of some invisible medium conducting and recalling thoughts:

I personally have found that it was difficult for a medium to give me a name when I was holding that name in my mind. A little later in the sitting room when I was thinking of something else the name was given correctly. We ought therefore in telepathic experiments always to make allowance for the possibility that ideas may be capable of being transferred to a percipient only when they have ceased to occupy the conscious mind of the agent.

Here, again, the time element enters into matters. How has duration affected the location of the name? *Is* it in the mysterious (unknowable by definition) subconscious mind of the agent? Or is it hanging in some ethereal space, gradually susceptible of perception by the medium? This theory of an intermediary ether, as Mace observed, is possible but, seemingly, unprovable. It would certainly account for telepathy taking time, as in the above case with Soal, but there are even more odd cases of people receiving thoughts from others *before* the agent has actually transmitted these. No invisible ether could harbour unthought ideas, surely, and it is thus a question of revising such imaginative theories if these events are to be explained.

The most famous case of a person receiving a thought before transmission is recorded in the 1940 annals of SPR, where Soal describes an insight of Carington's on his work, which has become something of a landmark in the matter of telepathy guessers looking ahead to cards yet to come, or at cards which had passed. The whole may be rather clumsily termed 'extra-sensory cognition' but not necessarily related to a time scale. Soal wrote thus:

Until the autumn of 1939 I still believed that it was practically impossible – at any rate in England – to find subjects who could demonstrate Extra-Sensory Cognition by guessing at the geometrical figures on Zener cards. This scepticism was not perhaps without its justification since during the past five years I had, without any apparent success, tested 160 persons and recorded 128,350 guesses. . . . last November my growing scepticism received a shock. The remarkable results obtained by Mr. Whately Carington in experiments carried out under rigorous conditions and with methods and material differing from my own were brought to my notice. . . .

Carington, as has been described on page 150, had discovered the 'displacement' effect. The guesser was scoring by getting beyond chance *not* the card which the experimenter was looking at but at a card which was one or two places earlier in the sequence. Soal found two subjects among his 160 who exhibited this 'displacement effect'.

It is perhaps fortunate for telepathy research that it was Soal, the specialist statistician, who publicized this effect outside time. In a maze of complex analysis he demonstrates that hits in Postcognitive $(+1)$ and Precognitive (-1) cards were beyond chance. He also observed that the chances of guessing were enhanced if cards of the same design were on either side of the card being transmitted. Here, indeed, seems to be fertile ground for future investigations.

It would be inappropriate to leave the topic of thought and time without reference to some of the more intriguing reports of coming events casting their shadows before. The idea of thought flowing in – of coming from some huge outer reservoir – is a common one. Our thoughts seem to *come* from somewhere. It is when they seemingly arrive from this strange somewhere and refer to events which are later found to be a reality that our attention moves to considering omnipotent beings directing our destinies, as hazarded earlier in terms of the pattern of life's warps and wefts. Are they but coincidences? Unlikely. Evidence, as I have pointed out before and make no apology for pointing out again, is, by its nature, independent, corroborative and cumulative. Such it is for the precognition of events, notably in the case of disasters. I shall content myself by giving a section of the best attested cases:

The Aberfan Disaster

At about 9.15 a.m. on 21 October 1966 some half a million tons of coal waste, loosened by rain and transformed down the years into a moving landslide, engulfed Pantglas Junior School in the village of Aberfan in South Wales. 28 adults and 116 children were smothered to death, this being a deferred human cost from scores of years of coalmining in the area. Appeals were

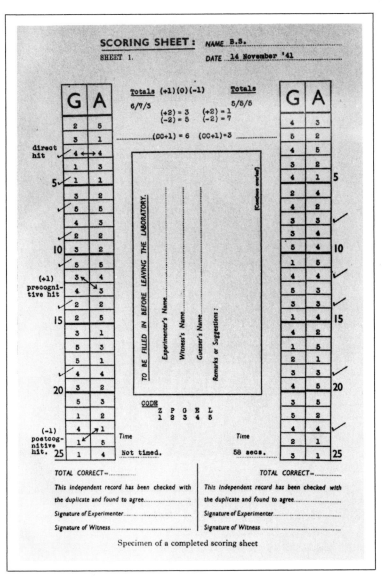

A laboratory record by S.G. Soal, emphasizing experimental rigour

Thought and time
Before the sinking of the *RMS Titanic* several people claimed to
have had premonitions of the disaster

made for those who would be prepared to record premonitions of the incident, and 60 were received and classified by Barker, Lambert and others, 36 of which being received in dreams. The earliest had been two weeks before and many vivid impressions were given, such as a moving black mass, hurtling trees being uprooted, and nauseating feelings of unease. The most poignant, if not the most dignified in human terms, concerns a remark made by nine-year-old Eryl Mai who mentioned to her mother, on leaving for school, that she was not afraid to die and that we would 'be with Peter and Jane'. When the children were buried in a communal grave her corpse was, indeed, laid to rest between her two friends.

The Titanic

On the night of 14 April 1912 the *R.M.S. Titanic* collided with an iceberg on her maiden voyage across the Atlantic. 1503 people died through drowning or freezing in the water, and 703 survived. In 1898 a novelist, an ex-sailor, named Robertson wrote an adventure story about a giant, unsinkable ship called the *Titan* which was wrecked and which carried 'as few boats as would satisfy laws'. Cheiro, the palmist, warned the journalist W.T. Stead, who perished in the disaster, that 'travel would be dangerous' for him in April 1912, and Stead himself had earlier written of an imaginary shipwreck in which a steamship collided with an iceberg. Again, psychics and dreamers had premonitions, but these were not systematically verified or recorded. Enough were retailed, however, to suggest that some people foresaw the event, as, for example, one Mrs. Marshall who stood on the roof of her house with her husband and family to view the ship passing near the Isle of Wight. She became hysterical at her premonition of the sinking and, even though she urged that action should be taken, was largely ignored or ridiculed.

The deaths of American Presidents

Several of these have been foreseen, notably that of Lincoln by the medium D.D. Home and Kennedy by the seer Jeanne Dixon. Krippner, at a drugs session nineteen months before Kennedy's assassination, hallucinated while in the psychedelic state that the event would take place. (This latter case buttresses the theory that deeper levels of the mind may discern the future, such areas sometimes being reached when under the influence of drugs or in hypnotized, meditative or clairvoyant states.) Garfield, Lincoln, Kennedy and McKinley are all alleged to have had presentiments of their own death.

It is clear from cases over the past century that warnings of dangers are often given at a sensory level and, that by heeding such warnings, the misadventures may be averted. One of the most interesting books on the subject was written by Maurice Maeterlinck, the Belgian philosopher and playwright, and is entitled *The Unknown Guest*. It is often quoted in contemporary speculations on time and thought, and is of particular interest in that the author writes imaginatively of the nature of our unknown subconscious mind, which apparently has access to some inner perception of future events on occasions. Significantly, the original title is *L'Hôte inconnu* and the word *Hôte* may be literally translated as 'a person who gives hospitality'. Such gifts are largely unrecorded in human affairs and, all too often, are sometimes wrongly ascribed to coincidence or imagination. Yet if, as Maeterlinck hints, we may benefit from listening to the promptings of our inner host, it is surely time that more sympathy was given to the many reports which have gradually accumulated down the years. Some of Maeterlinck's ideas will be discussed in Part Three, Chapter 1. There is thus evidence that the telepathic process (or state) often occurs outside our family day-to-day time scales. This re-consideration of theories and concepts in order to generate imaginative research and interpret findings is the theme of the following and final chapters in this book.

Speculations

1

Theories of telepathy

If telepathy savours of the vague and abstract, then attempting to theorize about it may be irritating for many. Theorizing smacks of arguing academics, often in some comfortable university setting removed from the workaday world, endlessly concerned with philosophical discussions or nitpicking unproductively at the meanings of concepts and words. Telepathy theory, to say the least, doesn't really seem to be of any practical importance.

In fact both telepathy and theories about it may be potentially of great benefit, for developed telepathy may be a rich form of communication between humans, and efforts at studying it belong more properly to the realm of treasure hunting rather than rainbow chasing.

Most new forms of communication met with hostility from traditional quarters when they were first suggested, for such ventures are essentially speculative (as is this chapter) and may result in a wastage of time and effort. Experts forecast that railway travel at fifteen miles an hour would be harmful; flying was thought to be fun and without any commercial future; the talking film was generally opposed; and the Postmaster General heartily debunked the idea of the penny post.

In the building up of public information about new ventures original ideas often have to be revised, and it is usually years before the steady accumulation of data brings about really useful knowledge.

What theories are current in telepathy, then, which might one day be of use? For, after all, if it is potentially a promising form of human intercommunication, we should range particularly widely and imaginatively in our quests for explanations, considering all theories and applying sympathy and critical analysis alike.

The most usual form of telepathy research in the past has been based on the theory that, at times, the contents of one person's mind may be consciously and silently willed into the mind of another. The model taken, popular in a century which has seen such spectacular growth in the physical means of communications involving electronics, has been that of the sender as a kind of transmitting station and the percipient as some form of receiver analagous to a radio or television set. Commonly it is imagined that brain waves somehow transmit specific shapes, pictures or numbers. Champions of formal ESP research on these lines would claim that they are making use of the only one which translates to a scientific experimental situation and promises opportunities for replication – a key feature of systematic procedure in the physical sciences.

However, there have been other theories and models. In terms of analogies thinkers have obviously been influenced by their times: Wallace, in the 1860s, favoured spirit intervention of some kind; towards the end of the century such scholars as Myers in England and Osgood Mason in America favoured explanations involving the subconscious or subliminal, as depth psychology began to take root; in the 1930s Upton Sinclair called his book *Mental Radio* when considering the exchanges between himself and his wife; Whateley Carington in the Forties, used the concept of the group mind, as conspicuously evidenced by Fascist Italy and Germany; and today there are models of bio-energetics (the energy field surrounding the body, as interpreted by some students of Kirlian photography) and quantum theories borrowed from physics which look beyond space and time for explanations of telepathy.

Such models are visionary and hard to grasp by those who would use them as experimental bases for research, in common with the most general theory of how telepathy might work. As a tuning fork can only be heard in air to carry sound waves, so it is suggested that there must be some arching psychic atmosphere to carry the complexities of words or feelings or images which form the contents of telepathic communications.

Such an extra-sensory substance is, oddly to many perhaps, by no means a new concept. In ancient China, for example, the concept of Ch'i – an all surrounding vitality or cosmic breath – has been accepted for centuries. We in the pragmatic West have no similar word, and perhaps Mesmer came near towards elucidating matters when he described it thus in the second of his *Propositions Asserted*:

> A universally distributed fluid, so continuous as to admit of no vacuums anywhere, rarefied beyond all comparison, and by nature able to receive, propagate and communicate all motion – this is the medium of the influence.

Sir Oliver Lodge also developed the concept of ether, which fulfilled an identical function. In the Victorian magazine *Borderland* (Vol 1. No 111. January 1894) he maintained in an article on thought-transference that the real medium of communication in the process was, in fact, ether. He drew attention to two experiments which demonstrated how both air and ether may be shown to act as modes of transmission. If two identical tuning forks are held apart and one is struck and vibrated, the other presently begins to do so, as sound waves impinge upon the receptive fork through the medium of the surrounding air. Then if two twin magnets are suspended a few feet from each other and one is swung, the other will swing also. Here the medium of transmission is ether, maintained Lodge, and the psychic activity of one mind directed to another may be analogous to the magnetic field around one magnet being activated by movement in the other.

In the language of the occult, the 'etheric' body is reckoned by some scholars to permeate and extend beyond the physical, and in his book *The Human Atmosphere* Dr. Kilner of St. Thomas' Hospital, London described such a surround in relation to his experiments of more than sixty years ago when he maintained that beyond the etheric body extended the aura, which served to indicate disease or health. He cites some eighty cases where he examined auras, using coloured screens, thus demonstrating the utility of the concept of the etheric body and the aura, both of which may be instrumental features of telepathic transmissions. His work has never been replicated and is generally ignored.

What of theories that telepathic transmissions make use of the subconscious mind or some unknown subliminal mechanism? In his book *Telepathy and the Subliminal Self*, published in 1897, Osgood Mason, Fellow of the New York Academy of Medicine, delivered a slashing attack on materialists who do not bother to consider his case:

> It is a truism that our western civilization is overintense and practical; it is materialism which values nothing that cannot be weighed, measured, analyzed, labelled and appraised; feeling, intuition, aspiration, monitions, glimpses of knowledge that are from within – not external nor distinctly cognizable – these are all slighted, despised, trampled upon by a supercilious dilettantism on the one hand and an uninstructed philistinism on the other, and the result has been a development that has been abnormal, unsymetrical, deformed and tending to disintegration.

More than eighty years later we may easily recognize how such attitudes have blighted our century, but such orientations, which tend to depress telepathy research and theorizing, are as old as mankind.

Mason identified the four theories to explain telepathy. Communication is through:

1. A vibratory medium between sender and receiver, analagous to the atmosphere, for propagating sound, or the universal ether for propagating light.
2. An effluence of some kind emanating from one of the persons concerned and acting as a medium for the time being.
3. A sixth sense.
4. A duplex personality or the subliminal self.

He queries whether 1. exists at all; he does not think that 2. 'would be capable of fulfilling the numerous functions demanded of it'; 3. one possibility in some cases; but he considers 4. to be the most fruitful area of study.

Others, such as Myers, Gurney, Sidgwick, Hyslop and the American occultist Henry Frank, all suggested that the unconscious self was active in both telepathic transmission and repetition. This last named writer, in his book *Psychic Phenomena, Science and Immortality*, maintains that the 'unconscious self is always active inversely to the activity of the conscious self'. From this it may be seen that in cases quoted earlier in this book, where the senses have been lulled by hypnosis or, in the case of primitives, by drum rhythms, then telepathic transmissions have been facilitated.

At this point it would be over-timorous not to attempt some form of synthesis of theories put forward over the years, especially within the context of a chapter marked speculations.

In this century there has generally been a shift away from brain-wave theories and research models which involved conscious willing and passive receiving; the assumed process of conscious transmission, too often taken for granted in the past, now is made problematic with the growing interest in parapsychology and a focussing upon concepts of meaning in such novel subjects as linguistics and sociology. How the individual reacts in depth to surface stimuli has become an important experimental focus, whether it be in the esoteric philosophy of existentialism or in merely listening to as many personal accounts as possible of various social phenomena. If objectivity was over-emphasized in the nineteenth century, perhaps it has taken our troubled times to restore some sort of subjective balance in the enterprise of scientific enquiry.

At a surface level, in spite of the earlier hostility shown towards Mesmer and Reichenbach, the notion persists that some kind of psychic effluence streams from living humans which may have some import in the telepathic process. This is not to be confused with the electrical impulses generated by brain and heart activity and registered by EEG (or Kirlian?) techniques, but is best summed up by Eileen Garrett's ideas of clairvoyance and telepathy depending upon active radiations, thus echoing the ideas of the doctors Elliotson and Mayo and other writers in *The Zoist* over a hundred years ago. However, not all by any means are able to discern auras or emanations, even by using Kilner screens, as is rather poignantly declared by the French scholar Sudre writing in 1956:

> Even after having sensitised their retinae with violet screens, psychical researchers like Rochas, Fontenay, and de Vesme, have not succeeded in seeing the aura. I have myself spent hours with Geley staring through dicyanine glass without seeing anything. It is true that we felt that with a little

autosuggestion we should succeed perfectly in seeing a mist where there was probably none at all.

At a deeper level, fanned by the brisk activities of psychiatrists in the western world, interest has never been greater in the subconscious in both symbolic and more specific terms. Clues to our real selves, whether in Freudian slips or Jungian archetypes, are keenly sought by growing numbers.

A simple point, culled yet again from philosophies of old China, is that we should cultivate quiescence at subliminal levels. As the base rhythms of the piano underpin melody, as emotional atmospheres support exchanges at all levels of verbal interaction, so might we observe the old aphorism of Confucius that 'Composure is of the essence'; in order, perhaps, that whatever subtle extra-neural activities govern telepathic processes are given favourable conditions to operate.

The concept of the importance of our greater selves is to be found in the writings and ideas of many: Paul Brunton writes of The Overself; Maeterlinck of The Unknown Guest; Dame Edith Lyttleton of the Superconscious Mind; Bergson emphasizes intuition, and Spinoza speaks of a certain form of knowing that is outside conscious cerebration.

For those who wish to move out towards twentieth-century limits in the matter of studying the subliminal, perhaps the book by Maurice Maeterlinck written in 1914 (see page 164) represents the ultimate in what critics would call absurdity and champions bold theorizing. In *The Unknown Guest* he devotes some 120 pages to detailing experiments with The Elberfeld Horses whom, he considered, were easily able to perform mathematical calculations such as square and cube roots without effort; by means of tapping hooves in various sound patterns they were able to transmit words and numbers, and the author sums up matters thus:

> I will not set forth in detail the many different proofs of intelligence lavished by the singular inhabitants of this strange stable. They are not only first-class calculators, for whom the most repellent fractions and roots hardly possess any secrets: they distinguished sounds, colours and scents, read the time on the face of a watch, recognize certain geometrical figures, likenesses and photographs.

These abilities, claim Maeterlinck, stem from contact with some superior subliminal level, potentially accessible to animals and humans alike. His somewhat poetic prose on the matter echoes ideas put forward on the subject of public wonder in the first chapter of this book:

> We all, unknown to ourselves, live in the expectation of the extraordinary; and, when it comes, it moves us much less than did the expectation. It is as though a sort of higher instinct, which knows everything and is not ignorant of the miracles that hang over our heads, were reassuring us in advance and helping us to make an easy entrance into the regions of the supernatural. There is nothing to which we grow accustomed more readily than the marvellous; and it is only afterwards, upon reflection, that our intelligence, which knows hardly anything, appreciates the magnitude of certain phenomena.

One unsung hero of telepathy research and theory was Leonid Leonidevitch Vasiliev, sometime Professor of Physiology at the University of Leningrad. His research activities extended from the 1920s to the Sixties, and his book, *Experiments in Distant Influence*, written in Russian in 1962, translated and published in 1976, is a major contribution to the literature on telepathy. Experimental work conducted over forty years is described in detail, and there is a very interesting and full last chapter concerning theories of transmission. The usual sad and grey story of totalitarian repression emerges, however. Vasiliev died in 1966, and in 1974 his associate Eduard Naumov was sentenced to hard labour as parapsychology generally fell out of favour, being declared 'a pseudo science based on mysticism and idealism'. Anita Gregory in her introduction to Vasiliev's book described Soviet attitudes thus:

> Now as long as Vasiliev believed he was substantiating the Caszamalli's brain-wave theory of telepathy, he was secure from any reproach of antimaterialistic heresy, and he was manifestly encouraged and financed in the usual way. When it became ever clearer that his results did not support the brain-wave theory, funds and encouragement withered away. The definition in the Soviet Encyclopaedia for 1956 of telepathy as anti-social and impossible, considering the time and the place, is uncomprising enough.

Whether any newer movements, with more liberal outlooks, are incipient or emerging is not known.

Vasiliev began his work at the Leningrad Institute for Brain Research in 1921 encouraged by the founder of the Institute, Professor V.M. Bekhterev, who died in 1927. The latter, at the time, was working with V.L. Durov, an animal trainer who believed he could pass on mental instructions to his performing dogs. Such preoccupations with such lower species borders on the bizarre, to say the least; however, many pet owners would swear to the effects of mental influence, and there are several cases of experiences involving non-sensory links between humans and animals.

Durov was an animal trainer in a circus who specialized in carrying out unusual tricks with dogs which involved no obvious signals; he was famous throughout the Soviet Union in the Twenties and Thirties and believed that it was possible for some people silently to transmit impulses to others. Having spent much time controlling animals with his will and gaze, he tried to do the same with humans, by many accounts. At the heart of his technique was imagining, vividly, whatever he wished to come about – getting people to turn round in a bus, scratch their ears or other parts of the head are common examples – and also concentrating his willed commands in his penetrating gaze. This idea of some magnetic force coming from the human eye is centuries old, notoriously in the case of the mutual gaze of love. Perhaps we may best leave it to two poets from different centuries to express this:

> I took one look at you
> That's all I meant to do
> And then
> My heart stood still.

> (Lorenz Hart)

> Our hands were firmly cemented
> With a fast balme, which thence did spring,
> Our eye beams twisted and did thred
> Our eyes, upon one double string.

> (John Donne)

Vasiliev, like William Barrett, was interested in the concept of ideas being transmitted, as well as actual words or other symbols in an agent's mind. He was also a believer in the exercise of the imagination in telepathy experiments, and many involved senders inducing sleep in receivers at a distance. Percipients clasped and unclasped rubber balls at regular short intervals and these were graphically recorded, so that the exact moment at which slumber was brought about was established. The instrument for recording times of sleeping and awaking he named a kymogram. Subjects amenable to hypnotic suggestion were chosen, and the sender was put either behind the receiver in the same room or in another room. In accordance with the philosophy of the great Durov, the sender concentrated his will and tried to imagine vividly the other person falling asleep. The following comments underline the scientific outlook of Vasiliev, for it is failures which he records, leaving it to the reader to infer the high rate of success:

> From 1933 to 1934, 260 experiments in mentally inducing sleep and awakening on the subjects Ivanova, Fedorova and E.S. were carried out; of these 194 were accompanied by kymographic registration, of the rest only notes were made in the usual way. Out of the total number of experiments (260) the mental induction of sleep failed in 6 experiments, and mental awakening failed in 21. This amounts to 10.4 per cent.

Vasiliev was extremely interested in the development of telepathic theory, and considered some critical statements, such as those by the American George Price, as unimaginative: e.g. 'If parapsychology and modern science are imcompatible, why not renounce parapsychology?' He also felt that some psychical researchers, by contrast with Price, bordered upon the esoteric, and that

> this mystical romanticism compromised telepathic research for many decades. But this romantic shell has fallen away and has given way to prose – to monotonous experiments repeated thousands of times with the scrupulous segregation of a few grains of telepathic 'wheat' from tons of experimental 'chaff'.

However, he came down firmly against the mystics, and suggested that imaginative scientific investigation of the energy which carried suggestions should be continued, but pointed out that such a force is not known at the present time. He quoted significant scientific opinion in support of this:

> Pascual Jordan, the German physicist and Nobel prize winner, and Dr. B. Hoffman, a former collaborator of Einstein, think that gravitational force seems to have a similarity with the force which transmits telepathic information, in that both act at a distance and penetrate all obstacles.

A fitting epitaph to our gallant investigator is to be found at the end of his book, which might well serve as a rallying cry for all who would consider mysteries of telepathy: 'I did the best I could. Let those who can do better.'

The notion that telepathy may operate within an acausal framework (independent of time and space and unconnected with our familiar physical world of cause and effect) was put most strongly by C.G. Jung (1875–1961). He had this to say of American research in his times:

> Decisive evidence for the existence of acausal combinations of events has been furnished, with adequate scientific safeguards, only very recently, mainly through the experiments of J.B. Rhine and his fellow-workers, who have not, however, recognized the far-reaching conclusions that must be drawn from their findings.

Jung goes on to point out that one experiment in 1942 involved transmissions between Zagreb in Yugoslavia and Durham in North Carolina, a distance of about 4,000 miles. Significant results were obtained, as was the case when a series of cards turned up at future times in the same sequence, thus reinforcing the time-displacement effect noticed also in England by Soal and Carington. Such experiments seem outside our concepts of both space and time and Jung concludes that we need to widen our imaginative horizons in seeking theoretical explanations. To do this, he suggests, we must meditate upon our subconscious selves, which may be tuned in to other spatial and temporal dimensions; such subjects as alchemy, astrology and a close study of dreams may be helpful for all of us in a better understanding of our deeper dimensions.

But whatever one may think of the seemingly mystical studies of Jung, it is apparent that new theoretical viewpoints to direct future research are needed. In a perceptive book entitled *From Anecdote to Experiment in Psychical Research* (1972) Robert Thouless, veteran psychologist, revived yet again the ideas of Professor Kuhn on the links between scientific (discoveries) and paradigms. Thouless writes:

> The situation which in the past has led to the overthrow of an accepted paradigm and its replacement by a new one, is the discovery in normal research that some fact or facts revealed by research are not such as the old paradigm would lead us to expect. These may be called anomalies: examples are to be found in the failure of the Michelson-Morley experiment to detect ether drift due to the Earth's motion through space, Planck's discovery of unexpected irregularities in black box radiation (leading to the quantum theory) the discovery of diffraction fringes which amongst other things led to the general acceptance of wave theory of light, and so on. In all science, the turning up of an experimental result that would not have been predicted from existing ways of thinking is important as a challenge to those ways of thinking.

In telepathy research, as we have seen, effects outside time and space have been noted as oddities. Further, the best telepathy data have been generated in the case of hypnotized percipients, and in primitive societies the induction of trance-like conditions by drums or dancing produces extra-sensory powers. Jung and many others have at least drawn attention to the subconscious as a fruitful area of study, and perhaps it may be left to the psychologist William James to sum matters up when he wrote, 'We live on the surface of our beings'.

If any experimental situation has yielded the true gold of the unexpected, a case may be made for the 'experiments' carried out by Russell Braddon and Sidney Piddington in Changi prison camp forty years ago. No doubt they were actively considering the commercial possibilities of a stage telepathy act, but at one point, when both were in the usual semi-fatigued condition brought about by forced labour and malnutrition and a lowering of conscious vitality, Piddington remarked to Braddon, 'I seem to be picking up your thoughts about half the time. . . .' Cynics will relate this to code developments; others to models of relaxed consciousness which facilitate telepathic communication; as Piddington came to say to radio listeners, '*You* are the judge'.

Meanwhile we might move on to consider the current experimental situation in telepathy, with all its multitude of measuring techniques – and the opinions of those upon whom such are imposed.

2

Current directions

If the founders of the Society for Psychical Research were able, in some phantom manner, to visit their on-going enterprise a hundred years after its founding in 1882, they would be pleased at the vigour and scholarship to be found at SPR headquarters. Interest in ESP has never been keener, and all age groups from many walks of life and most academic disciplines are to be found among members and associates. A glance at publications, cassettes available, and topics of current lectures reveals an awareness of the need for perspectives from all points of view and, saliently, the constant need for data, hypothesis and experiment. Academics tend to predominate as lecturers at conferences, and familiar topics such as apparitions, reincarnation, and the whole area of scientific investigation applied to extra-sensory behaviours and recordings are well in evidence.

In the field of telepathy, research is conventional; at London University, for example, there are experiments in EEG activity in different parts of the brain in relation to states of consciousness. Neurophysiologists, psychiatrists, psychologists and electrical engineers combine their skills in long-term experiments – currently the effects of transcendental meditation and EEG changes in relation to telepathy are being considered. At Cambridge clairvoyance tests are being conducted with staff and children, and the general humanity of the enterprise may be judged by an informal comment from Dr. Carl Sargent, director of projects, referring to the significant successes of children in telepathy experiments as opposed to adults: 'We got significant missing out of the staff and hitting from the kids, and a whopping great difference between the two . . . . P. 0005'. This means that the chances of the success ratio of children and adults being the same are in excess of 2000 to 1 or, in everyday terms, that some intervening factor accounts for the more favourable results from the young. This may be their sensitivity to the thoughts of others, a feature common to some children, as their mothers attest, on occasions. Here, indeed, is a very fruitful direction for current research, yet Carl Sargent is little appreciated in contemporary psychological circles.

What of the future of laboratory research in telepathy, making use of techniques and technologies from the physical and behavioural sciences? There have certainly been refinements in testing techniques, and much data, both for present and future research, have been accumulated, especially at Duke University in North Carolina where research has been going on for half a century or more, and it is instructive to browse through findings in the collected issues of the *Journal of Parapsychology*. A current glossary has relegated telepathy to but two lines, for it is now defined at Duke as: 'Extrasensory perception of the mental state or activity of another person.' It thus emerges as a special branch of ESP, and it is under this abbreviation that it is usually classified in most libraries. The term 'thought-reading' is now hardly ever used, and 'mind-reading' seems, oddly, to be associated more with stage telepathy, which is largely defunct.

The whole area of research into the paranormal seems to be growing more complex, especially in the field of telepathy testing. In an interview with Louisa Rhine in 1970, the psychologist R.H. Thouless remarked that, 'Experimental work needs experimental workers trained in experimental, mathematical and instrumental techniques . . . the main responsibility for active experimental research is likely to continue to rest on the USA'. He suggested that Britain had lost her position as 'the Mother Country of psychical research' because 'the leisured class has died out', and that the subject is not likely to find favour in conventional human studies. 'I suspect that a good many professors of psychology would not welcome such a development within their departments'.

Books and articles published in the past decade reveal a refreshing blend of detailed statistical analysis of run-of-the-mill experiments like card-guessing and dice-throwing, and occasionally the more outrageous, such as an experiment which involved choosing racehorse winners on a hunch-versus-form basis. (The sensitive's selections proved superior to those of a student of form. Few, it seems, have followed up this report!) Mitchell's much-publicized Apollo 14 card-guessing experiments have been reported in considerable detail, the results obtained being only modestly significant. It is difficult to pick out from the articles and books published recently any which would be unanimously declared as being of key importance in current telepathy research. Much of the work reviewed involves card-guessing, a run of twenty-five Zener cards being the most normal unit for measuring what is referred to as 'Psi success'. A consciousness of the need for sound statistical methods may be seen in many articles. Such difficulties as loosely controlled proceedings, poor definitions, misrecording, instructions not followed, 'fudging' and 'gross errors in statistical method' all of which emerge as pitfalls, as they have down the years in all sciences at all times and places. Such preoccupations have led to more sophisticated test techniques, and the cumulative volumes for each year demonstrate that Psi research in the United States has become a specialized industry with a language and methodology of its own.

Student volunteers are traditionally the largest group employed in in experimental work, although there are one or two excursions into the non-human area, such as 'Psychokinesis in Aggressive and Non-Aggressive Fish' and Psi learning in Rats'. Zener cards and pictures emerge as the most commonly used test items, but more imaginative and expansive experimental situations occasionally appear now.

The debate about the worth of telepathy research is waged by two traditionally opposed camps whose views are expressed by writers such as P. Diaconis in *Statistical Problems in ESP Research Science*, 1978: 'Modern Parapsychological Research is important. If any of its claims are substantiated it will radically change the way we look at the world'; and R. Hyman writing in *The Humanist* in 1977: 'If ESP were proven to be a reality it would not provide a serious threat to science or other accepted views'. Here, indeed, we are at the crossroads in telepathy research. Is it important? Does it make any difference? In view of the fact that effects are so marginal and the whole process generally outside human experience and inapplicable in everyday life, is it worth either continuing experiments or even considering telepathy (or Psi or ESP) any further? The labours of fifty years at Duke testify

Matthew Manning undergoing scientific control
The electrodes on his head are connected to a variety of appliances
to monitor the results of psychic phenomena

as to the industry of the researchers, but is it all really worth
while?

Certainly interest in parapsychology at academic levels has
never been greater, and some may say that this alone justifies
research. But if it is to be pursued there certainly seems to be a
case for suggesting that its procedures should be both more
imaginative and also more leisurely. To give some idea of the
way in which an individual might be tested for telepathic
powers, we might consider in some detail the experiences of
Matthew Manning (a leading British psychic, in his mid-
twenties) who underwent tests at the Washington Research
Center in May and June in 1977, and at the Mind Science
Foundation in San Antonio in October of that year and later in
January 1978. (Accounts of these experiments are to be found in
the *SPR Journal* for December 1979.) Matthew Manning has
gained a reputation for his outstanding 'automatic drawings' as
a psychic artist in the style of Picasso, Rowlandson and others,

his telekinetic experiences, and his dedication to healing. While generally tolerant of everybody, he understandably limits such research testings, and now prefers to concentrate on healing.

The report published by the Washington Research Center, *A Month with Matthew Manning* describes three weeks spent by Manning in David, California, and one final week in San Francisco. In its introduction Jeffrey Mishlove writes that, 'The report does not constitute a finished scientific product, but rather the raw scientific process itself, in its vitality . . . our errors and mistakes are reported here in order that students and interested non-parapsychological researchers can learn from them as we have'. The report is thus useful in outlining laboratory techniques in current use, and is also a frank document in which researchers disclose unsuccessful activities, a state of affairs found only rarely in much scientific research. If, as Wilde observed, experience is the name we give to our mistakes, then both individuals and organizations operate by trial and error; but all tend to disclose evolved techniques of dealing with problems rather than the errors, or even disasters, which saliently lead to these.

When Manning visited Japan before going to the States, during one of his appearances on television there had been more than 1200 accounts of glass shattering in homes which could not be ascribed to acoustical causes. The American investigators wondered whether such happenings would occur during his month-long stay in the San Francisco Bay area. In fact, minor unusual events did occur; high-pitched pinging noises after Manning had left one room; a key bent, a long-stopped cuckoo clock starting; a contact lens bent and later straightened; a video recording of Manning in colour appearing momentarily in black and white; and during a radio broadcast by Manning a dozen 'phone calls reporting unusual phenomena, such as taps turned off but water continuing to flow. It would be hard to dismiss all these as illusions, and the case seems well founded for Manning having around him some energy field which could be transmitted, with odd effects over a variety of distances. Certainly this was the explanation offered by those who had been in his presence and who felt that some form of psychic residue had caused these strange happenings.

Also in California, Manning took part in ESP experiments

which involved guessing whether canisters contained water, influencing the growth of radishes and rye grass by thought concentration, and perceiving target drawings. In all these he achieved significant results. EEG experiments were carried out on him to test the possibility of simultaneous brain-wave patterns occurring in agent and percipient, when the agent (Manning) in one room tried to influence the percipient (Fred Lorenze) in another. Lorenze wrote:

> Following a baseline period, and responding to instructions from Dr. Chapman, Manning sent suggestions to me to be wide awake, to go to sleep, to awake again, with rest periods in between . . . the correspondences between Manning's and my own were most dramatic . . .

The rather complex design of the experiment, which is explained in anatomical and electrical terminology, shows that patterns in occipital and parietal regions of the brain, (alpha, with associated beta and kappa rhythms) and the power spectra generated were very similar in the two. In everyday language:

> The similarity of Manning's EEG and mine was greatly increased as soon as he started to try and influence me at the end of my baseline period, and was maintained throughout the experiment.

These results demonstrate yet again that suggestion may accompany brain-wave patterns which are replicated in the brains of agent and percipient. In other experiments Manning experienced personality conflicts with investigators, or found electrodes fitted on his head painful. However, outcomes endorsed the sensitivity of the electro-encephelograph as an instrument capable of recording brain-wave rhythms in terms of alpha, beta and kappa waves. The experimental possibilities using EEG are thus immense, and are currently being developed, as in Professor Ellison's work at St. Thomas' Hospital, London.

The psychological perspective, often overlooked in the past, cannot be ignored. The ambience of the test situation, to say nothing of the feelings of the experimenting team, is of crucial importance. Eileen Garrett made an interesting statement on the subject in 1937 when she contrasted American conditions at Duke University under Rhine with those in England:

> The conditions at Duke are tense and emotional in comparison with those of Mr. Soal in London. I, personally, prefer the quieter methods, divorced from constant urging and 'suggestions', that pertain in London with Mr. Soal and I fell that my mediumistic powers would be given more chance to emerge in these quieter conditions.

In telepathy experiments this sensitivity of all parties to social atmospheres and to each other is a factor which has too often been ignored. In the cases of the Creery sisters and the Welsh Jones cousins, observers were sitting close by, watching for any movements or signals, and such behaviour must inhibit the exercise of any finer human propensities. Indeed, all mental activity calls for physical comfort and repose, to say nothing of emotional quiescence: just as the peace of a library is the best setting for intellectual activity, so should a quiet yet sympathetic atmosphere be present in telepathy experimentation.

Matthew Manning adds a very individual note to the end of the Washington Research Center Report:

> An important consideration which should be adopted in future work is the timing of experiments which, I believe should be controlled by the subject. This was not the case during these experiments and contributed, I suspect, to insignificant results on some tests which subsequently have been successfully conducted elsewhere. Since these experiments I have decided to participate in only three or four experiments each day which are conducted when I feel so inclined. Although this recommendation makes me appear to be a prima donna in some eyes, it has already resulted in significant results around 95% of the time. Too often subjects are engaged in one task after another with little consideration for breaks or rest periods; they are also expected to fit a nine-to-five routine with some researchers. Surely it is better to conduct three successful experiments each day than attempt twenty which result in non-significant results.

```
                    An informal worksheet drawn up by a father ( Mike Hague)
       when testing his son's telepathic powers.

       Jonathan Lindon Hague aged 7. D.O.B. 4.1.74
       Fair/Blonde hair, Blue eyes.
       Situation : Lounge, own house. Temp 65 degrees. Laid on carpet next
                   to my chair.
       Time : 6.30.p.m. - 7.15.p.m.
       Date : 11th February 1981
       Weather outside : Cold and rain.

       Observers   12 year old brother doing homework.
                   Grandmother acting as babysitter.
       Zener cards - 25.
       At his request :

       1st Run : eyes open looking at ceiling   T.V. on      5 out of 25.
       2nd Run : eyes open looking at ceiling T.V. off      11 out of 25
       3rd Run : eyes closed. Relaxed - laid down.          18 out of 25
       4th Run : bored, fidgeting, not taking much notice    4 out of 25
       5th Run :          as above                           2 out of 25

                   Grandma noticed within 4 cards he was getting the next
       card right before it was turned over and counted 15/21.

       6th Run. Promised the last. Very unsettled.           9 out of 19.

                   Then went on to play a game with brother and Grandma and I
       tried. 1 out of 25 guessing.with J's brother, 4 out of 25.Grandma Nil.

                   During their supper I took cards into kitchen. 10 were used
       at random. Jonathan in dining area when verbally requested what I was
       looking at got 7 out of 10 correct.   (signed) Mike Hague
```

Card guessing
A private record of an informal home experiment

Are young people today likely to be more or less telepathic than other groups? There may be a case for saying that the young are more psychically sensitive than their elders; in an age where working lives are shorter and lifestyles more comfortable, it is understandable that concern with the more subtle areas of human interaction, like telepathy, might grow. The unashamed interest shown by undergraduates in the occult, for example, may be an instance of this trend, and telepathic experiences are today more freely reported.

At a purely personal and anecdotal level I give below an account of such an experience by a young lady of twenty-five, Ms. S, an artist and an administrator. Her words are as spoken to me in a tape recording:

S. I went to the cinema with a boyfriend to see a film. I was about 18 or 19, the film was called 'Don't Look Now' and had been recommended by friends. The plot was involved and quite gripping.

About half an hour into the film, when I was sitting quite comfortably and absorbed by events on the screen, I heard what I thought to be the voice of my boyfriend. He was discussing various aspects of the film and the development of the plot. I listened to his deliberations at some length.

Q. What sort of voice was it?

S. Oh it was his normal voice. I didn't realise he wasn't speaking. I thought he was talking to me in a relaxed way. I remember that after a few sentences I had thought 'this sounds like internal thoughts' and I was comforted to think that what he had to say showed there were similarities in thought processes between people after all.

If I think very hard I would have to say that it was with an inner ear I heard it, not with the ear; it seemed to be near the temple, as though my temple and his were fused. The thing about it is that you hear things in ultra clarity.

Q. Were you surprised?

S. No. I immediately dismissed it, I didn't believe I was really hearing his thoughts.

Q. Was this the kind of stream of continuous comment that you might get from two women on top of a bus idly talking of the passing scene below?

S. There were similarities though his approach was analytical. I listened to him and developed my own thoughts alongside. I had heard friends discuss it and I had my own ideas on certain aspects. I was awaiting a chance to tell him my own ideas. After hearing a lot of his comments I said, 'Yes, but you know . . . etc. etc. . . . and Jane said etc. etc. . . .' This was the moment at which I realised I was hearing his thoughts because as I turned to speak and was still listening to him, I noticed his face was quite motionless.

Q. What was the effect on him?

S. He was absolutely flabbergasted. He hadn't been voicing any of his thoughts at all. We were both stunned by it.

The young lady has since had many telepathic experiences with her fiancé and also close friends, and differentiates analytically between empathic experiences with others at a distance and words and ideas that seem to come into her mind from those of others.

She has recently joined a study circle with others of the same age group and parapsychological interests, and it may be that such spontaneously formed groups will yield interesting data and ideas in the future to supplement research at an institutional level which has been carried along consistently over the past hundred years and has been faithfully recorded in various journals.

However, it is often the inspired individual who creates scientific breakthroughs, working on his own, under adverse conditions, and without encouragement or the support at all levels (these days computers and printing facilities are more important than ever). Pioneers of innovation, such as Baird in television and Whittle in jet engines, are examples. In the human sciences we await our innovators.

However, I would like to single out one modern pioneer, Tom Lethbridge. He came from the realms of independent scholarship, rather than any association with prestigious institutions, and was highly individual in his outlook. In his book *ESP Beyond Time and Distance*, published in 1965, Lethbridge expressed his dissatisfaction with modern science and claimed to have experienced many phenomena which belong rather to a fourth dimension. He wrote:

The scientific approach is now ingrained in the Western mind. Start at the very beginning: 'Strip off the layers' as Old Sir William Ridgeway used to say, and build up everything from practical experiment in the simplest manner. Bring in no unnecessary complications until the foundations are laid. This we have been trying to do; but it is far too great a work for a single married couple all by themselves in an isolated Devon combe. Still the isolation has a great advantage in itself. You can think clearly without being bothered by aimless tumult and din. . . .

Lethbridge had studied at Cambridge, was an archeologist and a tireless experimenter in dowsing, using mostly forked sticks and pendulums. He believed most firmly in the elusive energy atmosphere which many have thought to surround people and to be instrumental in sending ideas and pictures by the telepathic process. He wrote sadly of those who came holidaying to the West Country, referring to them as:

The wreckage from the cities, which washes up here from time to time. . . . When people congregate in large numbers, not only is there a continuous wearing down caused by noise; but there must be a perpetual sideways leakage, back and forth, to other members of the population, tending to lower them all to the rate of the most nervous and mentally inefficient.

The strongly vital are in danger of becoming psychically depleted, while those who are less vigorous are parasitic upon others. This, he suggests, is an unconscious process, perhaps a relic from times long past. He constantly refers back to early days and primitive worship and, like many other scholars, suggests that those in the Stone Age 'apparently knew more about the real meaning of life than the most erudite professor of science today'.

These views may appear unwarranted and rather familiarly simplistic. However, had Letherbridge anything to say about the transmission of thoughts or impulses between agents and percipients, other than the matter of some vital flow which marginally relieved the feeble and weakened the vigorous? He has little hard data to offer as a result of his research, although he is dogmatic as to the existence of telepathy. He notes that when he was an undergraduate at Cambridge the subject was totally unpublicized. Of successful instances of telepathy daily he writes:

> Thousands of people communicated thoughts every day without speaking. There is no need to prove it by cards and guessing games. It is as well known to the general run of humanity as that they have to breathe to live.

However, he asserts that the elusive psychic surround of Reichenbach, Mesmer and Sinnett does exist and that it may be empirically demonstrated. Although many in the past have spent fruitless hours peering through Kilner screens or purple glassed goggles in search of the aura, Lethbridge suggests how it may be discerned by dowsing:

> If you approach a person with the hazel fork pointing at him, it will rotate when the point reaches the edge of his psyche-field. As far as can be observed, this is about 24 inches away from a man and 29 inches from a woman. The force engendered by the meeting of two psyche-fields is considerable.

This elusive effluvia is fourth dimensional, claims Lethbridge, and may be transferred by humans to works af art they produce or, say, by a blacksmith to a horse shoe he is forging. Lethbridge's whole book, and others that he has written on ghosts, witches, and other psychic phenomena, point to extra-sensory links between human psyche-fields and many objects from the past, deeply buried and otherwise. He located mind and spirit in his human surround also, and thus endorses the idea of Sinnett as to the process of telepathic transmission being based on consonance between two auric human fields.

However, in spite of the work of Lethbridge and other dowsers such as Robert Leftwich, who has achieved highly successful results in commercial enterprises, the auric surround as a mechanism of transmission – or even its presence – is not recognized by scientists today, even though there have been attempts to surround subjects with artificial magnetic fields to enhance results, as in the Parapsychological Foundation in Washington in the 1970s.

It could be said that current research is being conducted by Saints, Sinners and Scientists. The Saints, inspired by a better world after life, believe that fieldwork in telepathy may eventually demonstrate the dual nature of man: that he is a creature not only of action and passion, of body and emotion, but also of finer yet more elusive qualities, which have variously been called soul, spirit, or even mind in the past; the old Greek idea of ingrained dualism, that we are as gods, divinely discontented, entrapped in animal's bodies, persists. For if telepathy is demonstrated there is the possiblilty that we may operate, often importantly, outside the familiar five senses; hitherto it has been considered fairly dangerous to venture into such seemingly mind-deranging areas; but perhaps newer philosophies are stirring.

The Sinners are eager that self-delusion should not prevent us from perceiving truth and for their interpretations have a vast history of man's mistakes to draw upon. The past is strewn with human follies, mis-observations, erroneous deductions and mistakes, many of which have led to a multitude of bloody disasters. There is a need, they say, to let the Great-Out-There take care of itself (for all will ultimately and personally be revealed to each of us in due course anyway) and to concentrate, coolly and logically, upon the comparatively Dull-Down-Here. They are especially attracted to the idea that folk see what they want to see, and look for outward signs of wonders and marvels to explain what might be mere coincidences or manifestations of the slumbering and as yet little known part of us which might be termed the subconscious or the subliminal. Furthermore, gullibility, ego-tripping and greed are often powerful monsters involved in the observation of much so called psychic pheno-mena; there is money, sometimes a lot of money, to be made in cashing in on occult areas; in a world where the only certainties are death, imperfection and change, there is a need to fly from reason and into some comforting psychic summerland which may ever be adjusted in design and intention to meet our human needs; whether it be in terms of establishing the reality of ESP or the likelihood of a happy hunting ground from which presences may project their thoughts to us. Many of this school, of course, favour the mechanistic (non-spiritual) view of man, or are agnostic in terms of higher planes of existence.

The Scientists, generally linked with physical science and laboratories, if not apparatus, are after paying homage to the gods, truth and knowledge. The old progression of measuring and predicting, as mentioned by Wallace, sums up their activities. Science puts its position rather starkly: unless observations and inferences are correct, there is no knowledge built up. Knowledge, involving predictive validity, works in relation to passing events or it doesn't. In the building up of knowledge by science the long slog from some inspired beginning seems to be the rule. It is as if man has to sweat at plenty of theoretical and practical nutcracking in order to extract some sweet kernel of truth, to be used hopefully, for the benefit of mankind.

Saints and sinners are in as brisk opposition today as when the SPR first started in 1882, when the latter very much dominated scientific opinion after the formidable technological triumphs of the Victorians and the denting of the theological beliefs of centuries by the Darwinians. Telepathy pioneers were thus driven to demonstrating that scientific rigour was maintained in their work, and this wish to establish honesty among telepathic subjects dominated. As Barrett wrote in the 1920s of the scientific climate of forty years before, much good data from the Creery sisters was not publicized because of their later tendency to cheat in tests:

It is right to say that, although I differed from them, Professor Sidgwick, together with Mr. Myers and Mr. Gurney, subsequently decided against further publishing of any of these experiments. They no doubt considered that at such an elementary stage of the investigation, with as yet so small a quantity of evidence to lay before so many hostile critics, it was absolutely necessary to shun even the appearance of the slightest contact with detected fraud. . . .

Today we are more relaxed, more tolerant of human imperfection extending to all areas of scientific research, and certainly more conscious of habits of thought and the need to extend these imaginatively. The structuralist debate at Oxford in 1981, querying curricula, demonstrates that students of literature are more aware than ever before that what society chooses for study might be made problematic rather than taken for granted.

It is not easy, of course, for our three camps to work together in harmony. Much of the literature of ESP in the various journals over-preoccupies itself with dogfights, usually between the spiritual optimists (sometimes known as vitalists) and the hard reasoning, no-nonsense rationalists. It is even less easy to see that all points of view have much to offer, but the Saints and Sinners represent the ever-present dichotomy of scientific outlooks down to the years: the impulse to create and the need for critical analysis. Both schools of thought have been guilty in the past of allowing their inner convictions to override what the data presented suggests: the Sinners look for deception (deliberate, unconscious and self-) where there is none, and the Saints at times ascribe purity of heart to charlatans which, of course, creates a demand for our third category, the Scientists. Scientists however, are too often disposed to use only one or two disciplines and should be prepared to consider more fully other perspectives: the historical and the sociological, for example, are sometimes sadly absent in much parapsychological research literature.

Perhaps this book might close with an endorsement of the views of Rhine. He was the outstanding pioneer of telepathy in our century and has been heavily influential in orientating establishment attitudes towards newer psychological directions in research on humans. He was also a spiritual optimist: his tradition is a long one and, looking back, such names as Mesmer, Myers, Gurney, Barrett and Carington are some who might applaud the words with which he ended his book *New Frontiers of the Mind* in 1937:

> Our merest fragments of discovery regarding the transcendental nature of the human mind are, in themselves, entirely too few and too little with which to map out the whole magnificent structure, but they are enough to insure the fruitfulness of the line of study. They are enough to lure

the explorer who is concerned about the destiny of man to follow up with all vigour and with every resource. They offer enough to warrant the hope that we may be entering upon a century of exploration into the psychical nature of man, spiritual as many will prefer to say, that may bring balance into our conception of things and a better foundation for living.

Select bibliography

ALEXANDER, R. *The Power of the Mind*, Werner Laurie, London, 1956

ANDREWS, V. *The Psychic Power of Running*, Thorsons, Wellingborough, 1979

BAIRD, A.T. *Hundred Cases of Survival after Death*, Werner Laurie, London, 1943

BAKER, ST. B. *Africa Drums*, Adventurers Book Club, London

BARBANELL, S. *Some Discern Spirits*, Psychic Book Club, London, 1944

BARKER, J.C. *Scared to Death*, Muller, London. 1968

BARNARD, G.C. *The Supernormal*, Rider, London, 1933

BARRETT, W.F. *On the Threshold of the Unseen*, Keegan Paul, London, 1920

BARRETT, W.F. *Psychical Research*, Williams & Norgate, London, 1911

BESANT, A. and LEADBEATER, C.W. *Thought Forms*, Theosophical Publishing Company, London, 1905

BODIE, W. *The Bodie book*, Caxton Press, London, 1905

BRADDON, R. *The Piddingtons*, Werner Laurie, London, 1950

BRAID. See Waite

BRANSON, L.H. *A Lifetime of Deception*, Hale, London, 1953

BRITTEN, E.M. *Nineteenth-Century Miracles*, Britten, New York, 1884

BROWNING, K. *The Science of the Emotions*, Theosophical Publishing House, London, 1925

BUCHAN, J. *Oliver Cromwell*, Hodder, London, 1934

BURANELLI, V. *Mesmer*, Owen, London, 1976

CANETTI, E. *Crowds and Power*, Penguin, London, 1973

CARINGTON, W. *Matter, Mind and Meaning*, Methuen, London, 1949

CARRINGTON, H. *Psychic Phenomena and the War*, Werner Laurie, London, 1918

CASTIBLIONI, A. *Adventures of the Mind*, Sampson Low, London, 1946

CHRISTOPHER, M. *Mediums, Mystics and the Occult*, Cromwell, New York, 1975

CRANMER-BYNG, L. *The Vision of Asia*, Murray, London, 1934

CRAWFORD, W.J. *The Reality of Psychic Phenomena*, Watkins, London, 1919

CROOKALL, R. *More Astral Projections*, Aquarian Press, London, 1960

CROOKES, W. *Researches and the phenomena of Spiritualism*, Psychic Book Club, London, 1953

CUMMINGS, E. *Unseen Adventures*, Rider, London, 1951

DAILY NEWS (ed. Giraud), *Ghosts in the Great War*, Fleetgate Publications, London, *c.* 1920

DAS PANDIT, *The Science of the Emotions*, Theosophical Publishing Co., Madras, 1924

EISENBUD, J. *The World of Ted Serios*, Morrow, New York, 1967

FLAMMARION, C. *Thunder and Lightning*, Chatto, London, 1905

FODOR, N. *These Mysterious People*, Rider, London, 1930s

FOWLER, G. *Goodnight Sweet Prince*, Consul World Distributors, London, 1962

FRANK, H. *Psychic Phenomenon, Science and Immortality*, Werner Laurie, London, n.d.

FROST, T. *The Lives of the Conjurors*, Tinsley Bros, London, 1876

GARRETT, E. *My Life*, Psychic Book Club, London

GIBSON, H.B. *Hypnosis: Its Nature and Therapeutic Uses*, Owen, London, 1977

GOFFMAN, E. *The Presentation of Self in Everyday Life*, Penguin, London, 1976

GOODMAN, P. *Growing Up Absurd*, Sphere Books, London, 1970

GREENWOOD, J. *The Wilds of London*, Stanley Rivers, London, 1874

GREGORY, W. *Animal Magnetism*, Taylor, Walton & Maberly, London, 1851

GRESHAM, W.L. *Houdini*, Gollancz, London, 1960

GURNEY, E. *Tertium Quid*, Kegan Paul, London, 1887

GURNEY, E. *et al*, *Phantasms of the Living*, Trubner, London, 1886

HALL, T.H. *The Strange Case of Edmund Gurney*, Duckworth, London, 1980

HAMMOND, D. *The Search for Psychic Power*, Corgi, London, 1976
HANSEL, C. *E.S.P.*, McGibbon & Kee, London, 1966
HASTED, J. *The Metal Benders*, Routledge & Kegan Paul, London, 1981
HAWKEN, P. *The Magic of Findhorn*, Fontana, London, 1979
HEINE, H.G. *The Vital Sense*, Cassell, London, 1960
HEYWOOD, R. *The Infinite Hive*, Chatto & Windus, London, 1964
HINTZE and PRATT, *The Psychic Realm – What Can You Believe?* Random House, New York, 1975
HOFFER, E. *The True Believer*, Mentor, New York, 1961
HOLZER, H. *Psychic Photography*, Drake, New York, 1976
HYSLOP, J. *Enigmas in Psychical Research*, Boston, 1906
JOURNAL OF PARAPSYCHOLOGY, Volumes 1970/9, Parapsychology Press, Durham, N. Carolina
JUNG, C.G. *Memories, Dreams and Reflections*, Collins, London, 1963
KILNER, W.J. *Human Atmospheres*, Kegan Paul, London, 1920
KLEISER, C. *How to Build Mental Power*, Funk & Wagnall, New York, 1917
Lancet, The Article on Mesmerism 29.10.1842, London, 1842
LAWRENCE, E. *Spiritualism among Civilised and Savage Races*, Black, London, 1921
LAYCOCK, T. *Mind and Brain*, Sutherland & Know, Edinburgh, 1860
LEAF, H. *What Mediumship is*, Psychic Book Club, London, 1938
LE BON, G. *The Crowd*, Fisher & Unwin, London, 1909
LE CRON, L. *Hypnosis, and E.S.P.*, 1970
LETHBRIDGE, T.C. *ESP Beyond Time and Distance*, The Scientific Book Club, London, 1965
LODGE, O. *Raymond*
LODGE, O. *The Survival of Man*, London, 1909
MCKENZIE, *Apparitions and Ghosts*, Barker, London, 1971
MACE, E. *Myers Memorial Lecture 1937*. 'Supernormal faculty and the Structure of the Mind', S.P.R. Proceedings, London, 1938
MAETERLINCK, M. *The Unknown Guest*, Methuen, London, 1913
MANNIX, D. *Memoirs of a Sword Swallower*, Hamiltion, London, 1951
MARQUES, S.D. *The Human Aura*, Mercury Office, San Francisco, 1896
MASON, O. *Telepathy and the Subliminal Self*, Kegan Paul, London, 1897

MAYO, H. *On the Truth Contained in Popular Superstitions*, Blackwood, Edinburgh, 1851

MYERS, F.W.H. *Human Personality and its Survival of Bodily Death*, Longmans, London, 1927

OSTRANDER, S. and SCHROEDER, L. *PSI Psychic Discoveries Behind the Iron Curtain*, Sphere Books, London, 1973

OWEN, R.D. *Footfalls on the Boundary of Another World*, Trubner, London, 1881

PANATI, C. *Supersenses*, Cape, London, 1975

PODMORE, F.*Modern Spiritualism*, Methuen, London, 1902

POST, Van der *The Heart of the Hunter*, Hogarth, London, 1961

Psychic Magazine, Interviews with Psychics, Turnstone, London, 1972

PUHARICH, ANDRIJA *Uri*, Futura, London, 1974

RAMACHARAKA, YOGI, *Psychic Healing*, Yogi Publication Society, Chicago, 1934

RAY, M.B. *Doctors of the Mind*, Scientific Book Club, London, 1951

RETALLACK, D. *The Sound of Music and Plants*, DeVorss, California, 1975

RHINE, J.B. *New Frontiers of the Mind*, Pelican, London, 1950

RICHET, C. *Thirty Years of Psychical Research*, Collins, London, 1923

SANDWITH, G. *Magical Mission*, Psychic Book Club, London, 1954

SCATCHERD, F. *Ectoplasm as associated with Survival*, Two Worlds Publishing, London, 1926

SHERWOOD, JANE *The Country Beyond*, Neville Spearman, London, 1969

SIDGWICK, E. *Mrs. Henry Sidgwick. Memoir by her Niece*, Sidgwick & Jackson, London, 1938

SINNETT, P. *The Rationale of Mesmerism*, Kegan Paul, London, 1892

SMITH LESTER 'Uri Geller' *Theosophical Society Journal*, London 1976

SMITH, W.W. *A Theory of the Mechanism of Survival*, Kegan Paul, London, 1920

SOAL, S.G. and BATEMAN, F. *Modern Experiments in Telepathy*, Faber & Faber, London, 1954

SOAL, S.G. and BOWDEN, H.T. *The Mind Readers*, Faber & Faber, London, 1959

S.P.R. Proceedings, 1882/3/4; 1900/01, Vol. XXXIII, Trubner, London, 1882–1901, 1920

STAVES, M. *One Sense Ahead*, Barker, London, 1971

STEAD, W. (ed) *Borderland*, London, 1894

STEAD, W.T. *Real Ghost Stories*, Steads Publishing House, London, 1921

SUDRE, R. *Treatise on Parapsychology*, Allen & Unwin, London, 1960

THORP, H.D. *Etheric Vision*, Rider, London

THOULESS, R. *From Anecdote to Experiment in Psychical Research*, Routledge, London, 1972

TOMPKINS, P. and BAIRD, C. *The Secret Life of Plants*, Harper & Row, London, 1973

TWEEDALE, VIOLET *Ghosts I have seen*, Jenkins, London, n/d

VASILIEV, I.L. *Experiments in Distant Influence*, Wildwood House, London, 1976

WALLACE, A.R. *Miracles of Modern Spiritualism*, Nicholls, London, 1901

WAITE, A.E. (ed), *Braid on Hypnotism*, Redway, London, 1899

WARD, J.S.M. *Gone West*, Rider, London, 1917

WASHINGTON RESEARCH CENTER, *A Month with Matthew Manning*, Washington R.C., San Francisco, 1979

WILLS, A.J. *Life, Now and Forever*, Psychic Book Club, London, 1942

YOUNG, M.F.D. *Knowledge and Control*, Collier Macmillan, London, 1971

Index

Note: numbers in italic refer to illustrations